NEW YORK

ART OF THE STATE

ART OF THE STATE

NEW YORK

The Spirit of America

Text by Nina Sonenberg

Harry N. Abrams, Inc., Publishers

NEW YORK

This book was prepared for publication at
Walking Stick Press, San Francisco

Project staff:
    Series Designer: Linda Herman
    Series Editor: Diana Landau

For Harry N. Abrams, Inc.:
    Series Editor: Ruth A. Peltason

Page 1: Commemorative fireman's hat produced by the Niagara Hose
    Company, c. mid-19th century. *America Hurrah Archive*

Page 2: *Looking Along Broadway Toward Grace Church* by Red Grooms, 1981.
    Marlborough Gallery, Inc., New York

Library of Congress Cataloguing-in-Publication Data

Sonenberg, Nina.
    New York : the spirit of America, state by state / text by Nina Sonenberg.
        p.   cm. — (Art of the state)
    Includes bibliographical references and index.
    ISBN 0–8109–5557–1 (hardcover)
    1. New York (State)—Civilization—Pictorial works.   2. New York (State)—
Miscellanea.   I. Title.   II. Series.
F120.S68   1998
974.7—dc21   98–14183

Harry N. Abrams, Inc.
100 Fifth Avenue
New York, N.Y. 10011
www.abramsbooks.com

Bathing at Bellport, Long Island by William Glackens, 1911. *Brooklyn Museum of Art*

CONTENTS

"The only credential [New York] asked was the boldness to dream."

Moss Hart, Act One, *1959*

New York is a state with dazzle power, whether you are gazing up at the Empire State Building or down from lofty bluffs at the Hudson River. The mighty boom of Niagara, the lush Catskills, Long Island's sweeping expanses of white sand beach: there is a certain swagger to New York's beauty. Human touches have altered the landscape only to enhance its drama—bridges, skyscrapers, a towering statue, and names in lights have made this state a star.

But New York has substance beneath its sparkling surface. On the cusp between Old World and New, this state has welcomed more immigrants than any other—in fact, 40 percent of current U.S. residents trace their American roots through Ellis Island. Countless newcomers have passed through New York en route to the country's heartland and far coasts, and many settled where they landed. From every wave of arrivals, New York has kept something. Its foods are Dutch, Chinese, African. Its language is seasoned with Yiddish, Spanish, Italian. Its architecture—well, it's all here, atrium to ziggurat. If New York is America's Old Country, it is also our fountain of cultural renewal, taking in the world and presenting it anew.

Just as there are many kinds of New Yorkers, there are many New Yorks. No state shows greater contrasts in geography and character than those that distinguish "upstate" from "downstate." The five boroughs of New York City cover less than 1 percent of the state's total area, but they hold the global spotlight. The Big Apple is the arts capital as well as the financial

Roosevelt Mural (detail) by Ben Shahn, 1936. Included in Shahn's mural of immigrants arriving at Ellis Island are Charles Steinmetz, Albert Einstein, and his own mother. *Estate of Ben Shahn/VAGA, New York*

capital of the world, and it sets the pace for America in advertising, publishing, fashion, and journalism. Beyond the boroughs, stretching north to Canada and west to the Great Lakes, upstate New York offers rugged natural pleasures and historic, close-knit communities. Its rivers and mountain ranges, vineyards and apple orchards, inspired America's first national artwork, from Washington Irving's *The Legend of Sleepy Hollow* to the sublime landscapes of the Hudson River School painters.

The contrast between city and country has grown sharper over the years, and New Yorkers embrace both. Projects like Central Park suggest New York's conviction that it can outdo nature at her own game. At the height of the Gilded Age, chronicled by Edith Wharton and Henry James, Manhattan was a garden of urban delights for those who could afford them, as it still is today. Those same titans of industry and finance left a legacy of mansions

Grocery store, Harlem, 1940. Photograph by Aaron Siskind. *Library of Congress*

and museums in town, as well as gracious estates on Long Island and along the Hudson River Valley. Around the same time, New Yorkers "discovered" the great unknown country to their north. The wealthy built "great camps" on the Adirondack lakes, and the turn of the century brought efforts to protect the Adirondacks as "forever wild."

Through the centuries New York has been a land of discovery. Writers perennially celebrate first impressions, like F. Scott Fitzgerald imagining "the old island here that flowered once for Dutch sailors' eyes." Photographs and paintings of New York City feature its bridges and skyline, symbols of arrival. More Kodak film is sold at Niagara Falls than anywhere on the planet save the Taj Mahal. Eastman Kodak had its beginnings when George Eastman brought his pioneering photographic techniques to Rochester and helped us discover the art in our own lives.

Newcomers to New York usually discover something in themselves as well. During this century, many visual artists ceased representing the visible world and looked inward for inspiration. Is it a coincidence that the art world's center moved from Europe to New York in the years after World War I?

Beaux-arts garden at the estate of Mrs. Whitney Blake, Westchester County. *Smithsonian Institution, Horticulture Services Division*

New York owes its stardom to a happy accident of geography, a steady stream of immigrant energy, and an ability to attract dreamers and doers. People come here to experiment, even reinvent themselves—to "make a brand new start of it." Or they bring long-held dreams to the place they think can make them come true. Upstate or urban, New York is a passionate place, and that passion has left a magnificent legacy of public and private works of art. ●

NEW YORK

"The Empire State"
11th State

Date of Statehood
JULY 26, 1788

Capital
ALBANY

Bird
BLUEBIRD

Flower
ROSE

Tree
SUGAR MAPLE

Animal
AMERICAN BEAVER

Shell
BAY SCALLOP SHELL

Gem
GARNET

Take one look at New York's official seal and you'll know this state thinks big. Three mountains, a rising sun, even the entire earth are held squarely in line under an American eagle. Liberty and Justice each raise an arm of welcome to ships that meet on a tranquil river. As the grassy riverbank implies, New York is proud of its natural resources and equally

Bluebird and rose

proud of having domesticated them. The Adirondacks support the world's largest garnet mine—yielding the state gem—and most streams run clear enough for finicky trout, the state fish. Forests across the state boast sugar maples, providing New York's generous maple syrup harvest and autumn's dazzling colors. The melodious bluebird sticks around all winter, for which New York honors it as

"Excelsior!"
(Ever upward)

State motto

state bird. Diversity-conscious New York celebrates roses of all colors. Apples and milk put a whole-some face on big business. And the beaver, the state animal, still inspires New Yorkers with its schemes to outbuild even nature. ◈

Stately Tunes

By a 1996 decree of the state legislature, New York's official song is "I Love New York," words and music by Steve Karmen, but here's what people really hum:

"A New York State of Mind"
"Autumn in New York"
"Give My Regards to Broadway"
"I'll Take Manhattan"
"Lullaby of Broadway"
"New York Minute"
"New York, New York"

"Niagara"
"On Broadway"
"Saratoga Swing"
"Sidewalks of New York"
"Spanish Harlem"
"Take the A Train"
"To the Fields of Onondaga"

Above: **New York's sugar maples bring syrup in spring and glory in fall.** *Photo Michael P. Gadomski/Photo Researchers, Inc. Above left:* **The great seal of New York was officially designated in 1882.** *New York State Dept. of Economic Development. Left:* **The Blue Note jazz club offers a neon tribute to the Manhattan skyline.** *Photo Mike Yamashita*

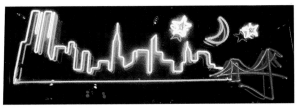

Thousand Island Dressing

Enjoyed from Wall Street to the West Coast, this mild-mannered dressing was concocted in the resort village of Clayton, New York, by Sophia LaLonde, the wife of a local fishing guide. It was popularized by a visiting actress from downstate, May Irwin, with the help of her friend, Waldorf-Astoria owner George C. Boldt—another regular visitor to the Thousand Islands.

¾ cup mayonnaise
1 tbsp. sweet pickle relish
2 tbsp. bottled chili sauce
2 tbsp. green bell pepper, chopped fine
2 tbsp. onion, minced
1 tbsp. lemon juice
½ tsp. sugar
¼ tsp. Worcestershire sauce
1 hard-cooked egg, chopped

Combine all ingredients except egg in small bowl. Stir in chopped egg last. Refrigerate. Makes 1⅓ cups.

New York's Victorian State Capitol, viewed from Empire State Plaza, Albany. *Photo Roger Bickel. Above:* The Empire apple, a new hybrid, was bred in New York. *Photo Barry Runk*

Why "The Big Apple"?

In 1921 a horseracing journalist named John J. Fitzgerald referred to New York City as "the big apple" of the racing circuit, the sweet dessert following bread-and-butter racing in the boondocks. By the next decade, jazz musicians in Harlem were referring to cities around the country as many apples on the tree, but New York as the one, the only "big apple." In 1971 the New York Convention and Visitors Bureau revived the slogan, little guessing at its power to jump from T-shirt logo to worldwide recognition. Today it represents both big-city temptation and the healthy state fruit.

Imperial New York

New York owes its nickname, "The Empire State," to George Washington, who predicted in 1784, while touring Mohawk Valley, that the state would become "the seat of empire." It was a bold prophecy, given New York's modest population, wealth, and status at the time. Still, Washington backed it with the purchase of 5,000 acres upstate for himself.

American Beaver by John James Audubon and John Woodhouse Audubon, c. 1840s. Hunted almost out of existence, New York's first commodity is protected today as the state animal. *Below left:* Atlantic bay scallops. The Shinnecocks of eastern Long Island made these shells into the finest wampum on the East Coast. *Photo James H. Carmichael, Jr. Below:* Nine-spotted lady beetle, the dainty state insect. *Photo E. R. Degginger/Photo Researchers, Inc.*

The Prized Scallop

How many states have an official shell? Algonquians were among the first but certainly not the last humans to relish Long Island's tasty bay scallop. Even more precious than its sweet meat was the fluted shell, which could be converted into valuable trade wampum. Stone awls were used to drill holes in the shells until Europeans introduced metal tools. Long Island wampum traveled extensive trade routes, as far north as the St. Lawrence River and as far south as Georgia. Bay scallops from New York now travel even greater distances to epicures' tables around the country.

Unveiling the Statue of Liberty by Edward Moran, 1880. Sculptor Frédéric-Auguste Bartholdi named his work "Liberty Enlightening the World" and sited it to face Europe in hopes that liberty might spread east from America. In this canvas, Moran depicted a glorious opening day—actually, it rained. *Museum of the City of New York.* Below: To raise money for the statue's erection, six-inch scale models like this one were sold. *Photo David Weingarten*

She is perhaps the most recognized piece of public art in the country, if not the world. The Statue of Liberty arrived in New York Harbor in 1884, a massive gift of hammered copper from France that has inhabited the dreams of immigrants ever since. Sculptor Frédéric-Auguste Bartholdi wanted to advance the cause of republicanism in his native France, where monarchists were gaining ground. When his sculpture arrived by ship—in no

fewer than 214 crates—U.S. supporters began to raise funds for a pedestal. Hungarian immigrant Joseph Pulitzer began a campaign in his newspaper, *The New York World,* and his ardent editorials yielded the needed $100,000—most in contributions of less than one dollar.

Visitors to Liberty Island can climb upward for 300 feet through an iron interior engineered by Alexandre Gustave Eiffel. At the top, thanks to a 1986 overhaul, Liberty's torch gleams afresh with real gold filigree, while her copper—once bright as a new penny—retains the patina of an eventful century. ●

"The New Colossus"

.... Here at our sea-washed, sunset gates shall stand
A mighty woman with a torch, whose flame
Is the imprisoned lightning, and her name
Mother of Exiles. From her beacon-hand
Glows world-wide welcome; her mild eyes command
The air-bridged harbor that twin cities frame.

Emma Lazarus, 1883

Above: Louis Comfort Tiffany designed a stained glass window to raise money for a pedestal for the Statue of Liberty. The window once hung in the offices of Joseph Pulitzer. *Columbia University School of Journalism. Right:* The torch and part of the statue's arm on display at the 1876 Centennial Exhibition in Philadelphia. *Hulton Getty Picture Collection/Gamma Liaison*

c. 8000 B.C. Asiatic nomads cross Niagara Peninsula into what will be New York State.

c. A.D. 1000 Algonquian tribes arrive.

c. 1300 Iroquois migrate from west, conquering many Algonquian lands.

1497 Englishman John Cabot charts waters near New York: first European land claim.

1524 Giovanni da Verrazano comes upon New York Harbor.

1570 Mohawk, Oneida, Onondaga, Cayuga, and Seneca tribes unite to form the Iroquois Confederacy of Five Nations.

1609 Englishman Henry Hudson, sailing for the Dutch, enters New York Harbor and sails up the Hudson River; Frenchman Samuel de Champlain enters Lake Champlain.

1626 Peter Minuit "purchases" Manhattan Island from Algonquians for legendary $24 in beads.

1652 First school in America opens in New York City.

1664 New Amsterdam surrendered to British fleet, renamed "New York."

1670 New York Stock Exchange founded.

1690 First Colonial Congress takes place in New York City.

1725 William Bradford publishes colony's first newspaper, the *New York Gazette*.

1775 Ethan Allen and Benedict Arnold capture Fort Ticonderoga from British.

1777 New York passes the first state constitution; Burgoyne surrenders at Saratoga.

1783 British evacuate New York City.

1784–90 New York buys extensive Iroquois lands, starting a westward land rush.

1785–90 New York serves as first U.S. capital.

1797 Nation's first turnpike connects Albany and Schenectady. State capital settles in Albany.

1799 New York begins to phase out slavery, which it will abolish in 1827.

1811 Manhattan establishes a grid system, dividing unsettled lands into 12 avenues (each 100 feet wide) and 155 numbered streets.

1825 Erie Canal completed.

1836 New York State Museum opens, the country's first state museum.

1839 First known photograph of U.S. taken in New York City.

1840 Irish potato famine begins a flood of immigrants.

1848 First women's rights convention, Seneca Falls.

1853 At the Crystal Palace, New York City hosts the first American World's Fair.

1863 Enactment of a Civil War draft incites riots in New York City and Troy.

1869 Nation's first advertising agency opens.

1880 Metropolitan Museum of Art opens; George Eastman makes first photographic dry plates in U.S. at Rochester.

1890 Metropolitan Opera opens; Jacob Riis publishes *How the Other Half Lives*.

1894 First U.S. hydroelectric plant opens at Niagara Falls.

1896 Statue of Liberty is dedicated.

1913 The Armory Show, an international exhibition of modern art, draws 100,000 spectators.

1927 Charles Lindbergh takes off from a Long Island airfield for Paris in the first transatlantic flight.

1929 New York Stock Market crashes, leading to the Great Depression.

1931 Empire State Building becomes world's tallest building at 102 stories.

1932 Winter Olympic Games held at Lake Placid.

1939–40 New York hosts a World's Fair, where NBC begins continuous broadcast of television.

1952 United Nations headquarters opens in New York City.

1959 St. Lawrence Seaway opens, connecting Lakes Erie and Ontario to the Atlantic.

1960 New York passes the first state minimum wage law.

1964 Verrazano Narrows Bridge opens as world's longest single span bridge.

1965 Construction begins on Albany's great "South Mall" for government offices and public art.

1969 Woodstock Music and Arts Festival unites more than 300,000 free spirits.

1976 U.S. Bicentennial brings pageant of tall ships to New York Harbor.

1990 Restoration complete, Ellis Island reopens as an Immigration Museum.

1998 Centennial celebration of the consolidation of the five boroughs into "Greater New York."

WOODSTOCK
3 DAYS OF PEACE AND MUSIC...AND LOVE

New York may be known for the steel city at its southern tip, but nature holds sway in the remaining 99 percent. From Canada to Montauk and from the Atlantic to the Great Lakes, an astonishing array of forests, mountains, and waters unfolds. The land took shape during the last ice age, when glaciers covered most of New York and carved distinct geographic regions. The Adirondacks span the state's northeast, a vast wilderness of lakes, woodlands, and Precambrian peaks. Atop their high point, Mount Marcy, the Hudson River begins as a trickle from Lake Tear of the Clouds. The river rolls south through the Catskills, gracing orchards, historic towns, and granite cliffs. Halfway to the

The St. Lawrence River harbors the magical Thousand Islands—actually about 1,800 of them, ranging in size from a few square feet to 22 miles long.
Photo Mike Yamashita

Atlantic, the Hudson meets the Mohawk River. Generations of Americans followed the Mohawk west, and along the way they passed dramatic glacial footprints such as the 11 slender Finger Lakes, crystalline gorges, and roaring waterfalls. The most famed of these, Niagara, channels water from four Great Lakes to the fifth, Ontario. The St. Lawrence River carries that water east to the sea, bordering Canada for hundreds of miles. Far to the south, Long Island stretches its gentle hills and glittering sands between the Atlantic and New England's shores. ◉

Niagara by Frederic Church, 1857. One of the country's first great tourist attractions, Niagara helped instill landscape painters with a reverence for nature's "divine architecture," in the words of Church's mentor, Thomas Cole. *Corcoran Gallery of Art, Washington, D.C.*

The Ancient Adirondacks

Vast and wild, the Adirondack Mountains host a precious remnant of the forest that stretched across this continent 300 years ago. The extent of its rugged beauty is still awesome; at 6 million acres, Adirondack State Park is two and a half times the size of Yellowstone, and the largest park in the country outside Alaska. Amid blue-gray peaks and glacial lakes is some of the oldest exposed rock on the planet, formed nearly 1.1 billion years ago and hard enough to withstand erosion from several glacial episodes.

By the mid-19th century, most settlers had bypassed this north country, leery of its wicked winters, dense forests, and seemingly untraversable mountains. Naturalists who charted the Adirondacks in 1837 found forests teeming with animals, 200 species of birds, and 66 kinds of fish. Among early visitors were Mark Twain, Ralph Waldo Emerson, and Louis Agassiz,

White-tailed deer buck. *Photo Gary Griffen/ Animals Animals.* Deer thrive at lower elevations in the Adirondacks. Higher up, pine martens and moose have made comebacks; even cougars, long thought extinct in the East, have been spotted. *Right:* Lake Placid is one of more than 2,300 lakes and ponds in the Adirondack region. It is the only U.S. site to have hosted two modern Winter Olympics: 1932 and 1980. *Photo Carr Clifton*

> *"It makes a man feel what it is to have all creation placed beneath his feet."*
>
> John Cheney, local guide, 1837

who theorized that glaciers had scoured the land. Loggers and miners followed, leveling two-thirds of the forest by 1885. In that year New York's legislature established an Adirondack forest preserve to guarantee that it remain "forever wild." Today wild country alternates with refurbished lumber towns, health resorts, and Gilded Age "great camps" in a pattern unlike any other American park.

The Hudson River— Logging by Winslow Homer, 1878–79. Artists drew attention to the beauty and solitude of New York's logging culture. *Corcoran Gallery of Art, Washington, D.C.*

"*I thank God I was born on the banks of the Hudson!*"

Diedrich Knickerbocker (*pseudonym of Washington Irving*), A History of New York, *1809*

The Hudson Valley, Sunset by Thomas Chambers, c. mid-19th century. *National Gallery of Art, Washington, D.C.* The first published American legends took shape from the pen of James Fenimore Cooper, whose frontiersman Natty Bumppo called the Hudson "all creation." A generation later, Washington Irving's Rip Van Winkle sat upon a Catskill peak and gazed down to the Hudson as he nodded off for a 20 years' nap.

The River That Flows Two Ways

Algonquian tribes noted a striking feature about the broad river that traversed their homeland: it flowed south toward the ocean *and* north toward the mountains. They named it "the river that flows two ways." No wonder Henry Hudson, who rode the tides upstream in 1609, believed that he'd found a northwest passage across the continent. In fact, for more than half its length Hudson's river is not a river at all but a fjord, carrying the ocean tides a full 160 miles inland on its 315-mile journey from source to sea. Hudson left dejected when his passage narrowed to a mountain creek. But the far sweep of this river would shape America's commerce, and the vistas from its shores would inspire America's first national art.

Over time, steamships gave way to railroads, and sleepy towns became fashionable suburbs. But vineyards, orchards, and quiet towns continue to thrive along the great river. Conservationists have brought landmark sanctions against polluters, and the Hudson is slowly regaining its natural function as a protective habitat for more than 190 species of fish, as well as great blue herons, great horned owls, and other fragile city neighbors.

"WE FOUND A PLEASANT PLACE BELOW STEEP LITTLE HILLS. And from among those hills a mighty deep-mouthed river ran into the sea....We rode at anchor in a spot well guarded from the wind, and we passed into the river with the *Dauphine's* one small boat."

Giovanni da Verrazano, 1524

Storm King on the Hudson by Samuel Coleman, 1866. The many moods of the river and its fertile valley convinced a group of 19th-century painters that landscape—American landscape in particular—was a noble subject. *National Museum of American Art/Art Resource*

Kindred Spirits by Asher B. Durand, 1849. On the rocky ledge, Durand placed two eloquent admirers of nature: his friend Thomas Cole and poet William Cullen Bryant. *New York Public Library. Opposite above: Autumn—On the Hudson River* by Jasper Cropsey, 1860. A Staten Island native, Cropsey was one of Cole's disciples. *National Gallery of Art Opposite below: Schroon Lake* by Thomas Cole, c. 1846. New York City Mayor Philip Hone proclaimed that "every American is bound to prove his love of country by admiring Cole." *Adirondack Museum*

English immigrant Thomas Cole took his sketchbook up the Hudson River in 1825, and returned to New York City to paint three canvases that drew notice from the day's leading artists. Cole rose to prominence as he continued to search for the sublime in the land before him, and he began to mentor younger painters, including

Frederic Church, Thomas Moran, and Jasper Cropsey. The "Hudson River School," as they became known, trained their eyes on the Catskills, the Adirondacks, the river and the clouds, striving to capture nature's "divine architecture." In the process, they gave a young nation its first internationally admired school of painters and a new pride in its natural wonders. ❧

Friends of my heart, lovers of nature's works,
Let me transport you to those wild, blue mountains
That rear their summits near the Hudson's wave....

Thomas Cole, from "The Wild," c. 1836

Between Sea and Sound

Right: The short-billed dowitcher *(Limnodromus griseus)* is just one of the 30 or so different species of shorebirds that feed and rest at the Jamaica Bay Wildlife Refuge on their way to and from their southern wintering grounds. *Below:* The common cattail *(Typha latifolia).* Photos Robert Villani

Long Island is one of nature's most glamorous recycling bins. The great Wisconsin glacier melted here about 21,000 years ago, depositing boulders and topsoil scraped clear from Canada. Swelling seas then shaped miles of sandy shoreline, achieving Long Island's fish shape just 6,000 to 8,000 years ago. Tides and storms continue to shift the Atlantic beaches, while on the leeward side Long Island Sound offers refuge to ducks, fish, sailors, and suburbanites.

Long Island's farms grew corn and grains for Native Americans, and today the east end produces wine grapes as well as everyday and exotic produce. The waters that today yield bay scallops and a plenitude of prized fish were once home to whales, which supported boom times in 19th-century Sag Harbor.

For New York artists, Long Island is a second home. In 1877 Winslow Homer led several painters to eastern Long Island in search of light and space, and painters still migrate to the scenic east end. The "Ashcan" group arrived in 1912 with a focus on everyday materials and, again, light. Artists of the 1950s and later found space for their visions in studios that ranged from beach shacks to futuristic architectural statements.

Sea-Beauty! stretch'd and basking!

One side thy inland ocean laving, broad, with copious commerce,
    steamers, sails,
And one the Atlantic's wind caressing, fierce or gentle—
    mighty hulls dark-gliding in the distance.
Isle of sweet brooks of drinkingwater—healthy air and soil!
Isle of the salty shore and breeze and brine

Walt Whitman, "Paumonok," from Leaves of Grass, *1891–92
The poet was born in 1819 in the farming village of
West Hills, Huntington Station, Long Island.*

*A Sketch of Montauk
Light, Long Island* by
Sanford R. Gifford,
1877. *Berry-Hill Galleries,
New York.* Long Island
has been a favorite
refuge of 20th-century
artists. Fairfield Porter,
Willem de Kooning,
Larry Rivers, Frank
O'Hara, and Jackson
Pollock are among
many who have lived
or summered here.

The First New Yorkers

Nomads crossed into New York from Canada about 9,000 years ago, part of a great migration from Asia that began after the last ice age. These earliest inhabitants were hunters, following herds of mammoth, mastodon, caribou, elk, and deer that sought the lush vegetation of lands newly freed from glaciers. Few traces remain of these peoples—just some fluted projectile points. "Archaic Indians" followed: from about 3500 to 1000 B.C. these people learned to use native plants and animals, carved stone tools sharp enough to fell trees, made stone cookware, and experimented with pottery. Later tribes of the "woodland stage" flourished until Europeans overran their homelands, settling lowlands close to streams, rivers, and bays, using water routes for trade. While the men

focused on hunting and fishing, women cultivated communal fields. These tribes developed complex styles of pottery and decoration and devoted much attention to village life. Algonquian tribes arriving around A.D. 1000 included the Mohicans, Delawares, and Montauks. They were mostly supplanted by more aggressive tribes coming from the west a few centuries later: the Senecas, Cayugas, Onondagas, Oneidas, and Mohawks. In 1570 these latter tribes united to form the Iroquois Confederacy of Five Nations; this sophisticated alliance gave them an edge in stability, trade, and power over every other Northeast group.

I am turtle,
and my tribes remain forever countless,
from the day I first raised my head
to gaze back upon the horn of my body,
    and my head was a sun,
        and Creation breathed life upon the seed
        and four times, and again four times,
    I wept for joy at the birthing of my tribes,
        and chanted Creation for the glory
    of all these wondrous days....

Peter Blue Cloud (Mohawk), from "Turtle," 1976

Treaties in Beads

In place of written documents, the Iroquois wove details of business and diplomacy into beads. The formation of the Iroquois Confederacy was recorded in a "circle wampum"—50 strings of wampum, representing 50 chiefs of the confederacy, arranged into a round belt. The long-stable Iroquois Confederacy is believed to have influenced the writing of the U.S. Constitution.

"This is a very good land to fall with and a pleasant land to see."

Robert Juet, an officer on Henry Hudson's ship, the Half Moon, *1609*

Giovanni da Verrazano sailed his *Dauphine* into New York Harbor in 1524 and cautiously dropped anchor before entering the narrow straits that now bear his name. The Florentine navigator "found the country…well-peopled, the inhabitants…being dressed out with the feathers of birds of various colors." Henry Hudson got a closer look at land and natives when he sailed the *Half Moon* through the bay and up the river in 1609. Algonquian traders bearing beaver and mink furs marveled at blankets, iron kettles, guns, and liquor. A longstanding desire for each other's goods took hold; trade, violence, and warring alliances shaped New York's history for the next 150 years. ◆

A New World of Goods

Dutch businessmen formed the West India Company to secure the New World's riches and sent settlers to trap or trade for furs in the land they named "New Netherland." They established contact with the Iroquois, who controlled the fur trade, and the Dutch merchants prospered. Emigrants at first were few, and colonial governors were told to accept all newcomers, regardless of their background. By 1664 farmers had cleared land in "New Amsterdam," which would become New York City's five boroughs, fanning out to Long Island and up the Hudson Valley. Forts and fur-trading posts on the Hudson and Mohawk Rivers marked frontiers, beyond which Indians, the French, and wilderness threatened.

Portrait of Peter Stuyvesant, attributed to Henri Couturier, c. 18th century. Stuyvesant ran the colony from 1647 to 1664, and, in letters to the ruling Dutch company, pointed with despair to the settlers' diversity—the very quality that would define the future state. New-York Historical Society Below: Van Bergen Overmantel (detail), attributed to John Heaten, c. 1733. New York State Historical Association, Cooperstown. Opposite: Arrival of the Half-Moon, Hudson's Ship, in the Bay of New York in September of 1609 by Frederic A. Chapman, c. 1850, chromolithograph, 1868. At first contact, Europeans and Native Americans viewed each other with hope for material gain. *Library of Congress*

The Surrender of General Burgoyne at Saratoga by John Trumbull, 1821. National Geographic Society. Opposite above: Alexander Hamilton in the Uniform of the New York Artillery by Alonzo Chappel, c. 1776. Opposite below: Evacuation Day stoneware jug, probably New York City, 1783–1820. Both, Museum of the City of New York

Revolutionary New York

The Dutch lost control of their colony in 1664 to England, which renamed it "New York" in honor of James, Duke of York. New York prospered under English rule and was slow to favor revolution. But the cries of other colonies—and their own increasing taxes—aroused citizens' passions. The colony held strategic points, including Fort Ticonderoga in the north and the Atlantic port in the south—and became a major theater of the war; one out of three battles was fought on its soil. George Washington arrived in Manhattan in 1776 and watched warily as Britain's General Howe amassed ships in New York

Harbor. Would they head south to Philadelphia or north to Albany? Meanwhile, northern New Yorkers fought to delay General Burgoyne, who was advancing south from Montreal. With the Iroquois's help, the British captured Ticonderoga and closed in on Albany, but exhausted themselves in the process. Burgoyne's surrender to Benedict Arnold at Saratoga turned the tide of the war. Legend has it that when Burgoyne first sent word of surrender, his messenger delayed the news for 10 minutes while praising the splendor of autumn foliage along the Hudson.

"Get into the City. There, in the best manner possible,

learn the designs of the Enemy.

Whether they mean to evacuate New York wholly in part,

or continue the Army there....

Whether any Troops have been Imbarked lately and for what place.

Whether any have arrived from England lately, or are expected.

Whether the Merchants who came from Europe and those who

have been attached to Government are packing up or selling

off their goods...."

George Washington, "Instructions to Spies Going into New York," September 1780

Deck figure from the ship *Albany*, c. 1831. New York's frontier days coincided with the state's rise to riches, as 19th-century ships unloaded a growing stream of goods and immigrants at America's premier port. *Museum of the City of New York Helga Photo Studio*

Statehood brought no instant growth to New York. It was only the fifth most populous state in 1790, and it lacked a direct means to wealth such as the tobacco and cotton that grew farther south. Its biggest claim to national fame was its port—but the same could be said for Boston or Baltimore. New York made its big move in 1825 with the opening of the Erie Canal. By extending the Mohawk River west to Lake Erie, entrepreneurs opened a passage between the Atlantic and the midwestern frontier— with New York as international gatekeeper. The port surged to prominence and a stream of goods and people began moving through the state. Boomtowns appeared along the banks of the canal: Troy, Albany, Rome, Utica, Syracuse, Rochester, and Buffalo. Settlers in boats and stagecoaches migrated through the river valleys, some dropping roots and some pushing on west. Log cabins and tall tales sprang up along the state's northern and western frontiers. Meanwhile, the port of New York was learning to oversee enterprise of worldwide importance. By 1830 New York had become the nation's richest, most populous state. ●

"WHAT PLEASURE; WHAT RAPTURES WE ENJOY IN contemplation of a cleared, fenced acre of the first crop of corn, wheat or grass, that ever covered that spot, since the creation!"

Francis Adriaen Van der Camp,
Dutch settler in Barneveld, north of Utica, 1795

Let old men talk of courage bold,
Of battles fought in days of old
Ten times as bad; but none, I ween,
Can match a bear-fight up in Keene.

Keene Valley rhyme, 1840

Erie Canal Celebration, New York **by Anthony Imbert, 1825. Ship traffic was boosted by the digging of the Erie Canal, which linked the Midwest to the ocean and interior New York to international commerce. Opening day brought cannon fire and crowds to witness the maritime spectacle.** *Museum of the City of New York*

The Bay and Harbor of New York by Samuel B. Waugh, c. 1855. *Museum of the City of New York* Immigrants disembark at Castle Garden, the landing point that predated Ellis Island. *Opposite above:* Antonio Magnani with his sons on Ellis Island in 1950. *Photo Edward Hausner/The New York Times. Opposite below:* Poster for England's National Line, advertising departures for New York. *Peabody Essex Museum*

New York has welcomed more immigrants than any other American port. The first great wave began in the 1840s, when Irish farmers fled failed potato crops. Germans and other northern Europeans followed as revolution swept Europe in 1848, and by 1855 foreign-born residents outnumbered natives in New York City, Albany, and Buffalo. At first arrivals were routed through an old fort on Manhattan's southern tip, but by 1890— 7.6 million immigrants later—"Castle Garden" was overwhelmed. Federal officials took over immigration in 1890 and bought an island then popular for oyster picnics. The age of Ellis Island had begun. Between 1892 and 1932, more than 16 million people entered the United

States here—roughly 80 percent of the national total. Most were European, young, and exhausted from days in steerage. They faced a litany of questions from inspectors: Evidence of infectious disease or insanity? Experience as an anarchist or polygamist? Thirty dollars in pocket? Most passengers were allowed onto the ferry for the short journey to a new life. In 1954 the station at Ellis Island closed down, but in 1990 it reopened as a museum. The restored halls echo once more with voices and images of hope. ◆

"ON NOVEMBER 10, AT SIX IN THE MORNING, we finally made it into New York Harbor. I remember vividly being choked with emotion. I saw all these skyscrapers lit up. It was dark. It was wintertime. Little jewels, little twinkles, and the Statue of Liberty. Quite different than what I expected. To me, America was…a wild country of cowboys and Indians. In fact, on my tenth birthday in Germany, I got a cowboy hat from my uncle in New York. I did not think they had civilized life here. I thought it would be like it was in 1492."

David Froelich, emigrated 1939, age 11, on the Veedam from Holland

New York is lucky in its natural resources, though it sometimes pushed its luck too far. The beaver supply once seemed boundless, and the Hudson and Mohawk Rivers apparently ran to the center of the continent. The 19th-century seas promised infinite fishing and whaling. But in each case, nature gave out before New York was done reaping profit. The disappearance of the native beaver around 1700 forced traders to explore new directions. In the case of the Erie Canal,

good thinking and hard labor stretched the river resource an extra 363 miles. Sometimes New Yorkers found a way to profit from the resources of others, as when New York shippers dominated the southern cotton market. And often they dreamed up something truly new. George Eastman brought his dry-plate photography technique to Rochester and launched the modern photo industry. Isaac Singer perfected the sewing machine in a Cayuga County workshop and so transformed the garment business. By 1850, a third of all U.S. patents had gone to New Yorkers. And if there's one thing the Empire State likes as much as good ideas, it's the grit that turns them into fortunes. ●

Left: Acrobats Vase by Pavel Tchelitchew for Steuben Glass, 1939. Corning Museum of Glass Below: The Ice Cart by Nicolino Calyo, c. 1840. Museum of the City of New York. Opposite above: The Tontine Coffee House by Francis Guy, c. 1797. New York's maritime bustle carried over to its streets. New-York Historical Society. Opposite below: George Eastman using a No. 2 Kodak aboard the S.S. Gallia, 1890, photographed by an aide with the same model. George Eastman House

Cider Making on Long Island by William M. Davis, c. 1870. *New York State Historical Association, Cooperstown Below:* Bull weathervane, Dutchess County, c. 1885. *America Hurrah Archive*

Autumn Harvest

New York apples, cherries, maple syrup, and milk sweeten America's table. With a quarter of the state's land under cultivation, farming remains a vital part of the economy. Milk accounts for half the agricultural product, and New York is among the nation's top producers of both dairy and apples. Until the Civil War, New York was a mostly agrarian state, with settlers fanning out from Manhattan to farm the river valleys. Thanks to the Erie Canal, the Genessee Valley enjoyed a brief moment as America's granary before wheat from the prairie states won out. Many upstate farmers then opened their fields to cattle. And ever since records have been kept, New York has ranked an honorable second in U.S. wine production after California.

Atlantic Gateway

Henry Hudson—a ship captain, after all—recognized that New York's harbor was something special. A few short miles from open ocean, it provided shelter; myriad connections to rivers, estuaries, and bays; and hundreds of miles of usable waterfront. The port bustled throughout colonial history, bearing settlers, merchants, pirates, slaves, English fleets, and later the burgeoning trade of a young nation. New York's central location between Maine and Florida made it a focal point in domestic trade. Between 1815 and 1915, more than half of all U.S. imports passed through New York Harbor. Neighboring New Jersey once squabbled with New York over rights to the port, but later the two states formed the first interstate agency; the Port Authority still oversees the region's web of bridges, tunnels, railroads, and 4,500 ship calls each year.

Men of the Docks by George Bellows, 1912. Like his fellow Ashcan painters, Bellows documented the human drama of daily life in New York City. In 1998, Jan Morris reflected "It is hard to remember nowadays the permanent display that was the waterscape of New York in those days. The sea traffic was incessant, night and day, wherever you looked...." *Maier Museum of Art, Lynchburg, Virginia*

Midtown Manhattan may seem distant from the sounds and smells of the sea—but ascend a skyscraper or walk far enough in any direction and you'll see that it's still an island of "river light," in New York writer John Cheever's phrase, and that tugboats still have plenty of work to do.

"*The trouble with New York is it's so convenient to everything I can't afford.*"

Jack Benny

Rags to Riches

Donna Karan, Claire McCardell, Norman Norell, Halston: designers have congregated around New York's Seventh Avenue for decades. They owe much to an earlier New Yorker, Isaac M. Singer, who developed the first reliable sewing machine at his upstate workshop in Port Byron. His company designed plush showrooms to overcome Victorian skepticism about machines for ladies, and offered the devices with artfully engraved iron stands—"a beautiful ornament in the parlor or boudoir." When commercial models followed, textile production moved

Illustration from *Vogue*, 1920, associates European chic with a growing New York skyline and fashion industry. Among a bounty of spring fabrics on offer: "duvetine and twill," "supple wools," and "gleaming silk...to brighten the world." *Courtesy Condé Nast Publications*

almost overnight from sitting rooms to factories, with women as operators. For the Civil War, factories in Elmira produced uniforms; Rochester filled vast orders for boots and shoes; and New York City began employing immigrants throughout the garment industry. Its port brought in yard goods as well

New York designer James Galanos with model Carol Alt wearing one of his creations, 1983. *Photograph by Francesco Scavullo Courtesy the artist Opposite below: A* mother and her daughter display their early model Singer, hailed by *Godey's Ladies Book* as "the Queen of Inventions." *Singer Sewing Machine Company*

as passengers savvy to new styles from London and Paris.

By the 1920s, the "new woman" wanted a new look, and New York provided it. Fashion magazines flew from Madison Avenue into America's heartland, and garments followed by rail and truck. Though competition now is worldwide, still no one can match the critical mass of garment workers in 21 square blocks of Manhattan, where buzz on the streets becomes dresses in the showroom in a New York minute.

The Image Makers

By the late 19th century America had become, for many, the land of plenty. But as factories churned out production, a new problem emerged: what if no one really needed what they were selling? Enter the advertising industry. A few maverick wordsmiths and graphic artists gathered in turn-of-the-century New York City to think about what people would buy—and buy again. If they didn't want face cream, they surely wanted youth. If they grew tired of mint mouthwash or French soap, they never stopped wanting success—or its trappings. With clever words and sophisticated images, ad men turned America's yen for self-improvement into a passion for consumption. Meanwhile, from the same stretch of Madison Avenue arose magazines to define our image of beauty (*Vogue* and *Vanity Fair*), culture (*The New Yorker*), and success (*Fortune*). Commercial photographers created the fashion shot. New York's editors and writers even shaped the way Americans spoke and wrote—think of Hemingway's stories in *Esquire* or E. B. White's classic *The Elements of Style*. Here as nowhere else, the realms of ideas and commerce conjoin to create a cultural blueprint for the nation.

The man in the Hathaway shirt

I sit in an office at
   244 Madison Avenue,
And say to myself, You have
   a responsible job, havenue?
Why then do you fritter away
   your time on this doggerel?
If you have a sore throat
   you can cure it by using
   a good goggeral.

   Ogden Nash
in "Spring Comes to Murray Hill," 1931
The master of light verse worked as an
ad copywriter for a time. This was his
first contribution to The New Yorker,
whose staff he later joined.

New York's motto "Ever upward!" is made manifest in the steel and glass skyscrapers of Manhattan. By the 1880s, New York was amassing wealth and power, and its corporate giants wanted a concrete measure of might. Among the mechanical inventions that opened the skies was Elisha Graves Otis's steam-powered elevator. Steel beams, lighter and stronger than iron, allowed the internal frame that defines the skyscraper. Central heating, plumbing, ventilation, fireproofing: each marked an engineering milestone. Industrialists didn't care about such details; they just wanted their building to be high, higher, highest. F. W. Woolworth briefly held the prize when his 60-story flagship opened in 1913. In 1929 it was edged out by the Art Deco

Manhattan's glaciated bedrock proved ideal for bearing the weight of skyscrapers. Here, the famed midtown profile is seen from the New Jersey shore of the Hudson. At far right is the Empire State Building. *Photo Perry Alan Werner Right:* The Chrysler Building's Art Deco detail and celebration of the Machine Age remain a showstopper long after the sponsoring company moved out. *Photo Mike Yamashita*

Chrysler Building, itself soon surpassed by the iconic Empire State Building. Manhattan lost its "tallest" crown to Chicago in the 1970s, but it still displays the world's grandest concentration of tall towers—from Park Avenue's Seagram Building, a landmark of the International Style, to the twin behemoths (110 stories each) of the World Trade Center downtown.

"[THE SKYSCRAPER] IS TO THE nation what the white church spire is to the village—the visible symbol of aspiration and faith, the white plume saying that the way is up."

E. B. White, "Here Is New York," 1955

"THE CARDINAL QUESTION ASKED of every traveler on his arrival is: 'What do you think of New York?' Coolly I replied: 'The skyscrapers are too small.'…"

Le Corbusier, "The Fairy Catastrophe," 1936

Radiator Building, Night, New York by Georgia O'Keeffe, 1927. After moving to New York City early in her career, O'Keeffe became fascinated with the futuristic lines and lights of skyscrapers. From the high-altitude apartment she shared with her husband, Alfred Stieglitz, she painted neighboring buildings as a study in geometrics. *Fisk University Galleries and Collections, Nashville*

Bird's-Eye View of Trinity Church, New York. Drawn and lithographed by John Forsyth and E. W. Mimee, 1847. *Museum of the City of New York* The original church on this site (at which Wall Street begins) burned in 1776 and was replaced in 1846 by a landmark Gothic building by English architect Richard Upjohn. *Below:* Catalogue advertisement for Oneida Silver, 1924. John Humphrey Noyes founded the Oneida community in 1848.

"You may…shut your eyes, at least not force people's consciences but allow every one to have his own belief, as long as he behaves quietly and legally." So wrote the Dutch West India Company in 1654 to Peter Stuyvesant, who was trying to expel a group of Portuguese Jews. The company needed settlers, and religious refugees needed shelter. So Protestant Walloons came, unwelcome in Catholic France. Puritans cast out of New England came, including the Rev. John Throgmorton (who settled Throg's Neck) and Anne Hutchinson with her "antinomian" followers. And 23 Jews, fleeing Portuguese conquest in Brazil, survived attack by pirates to establish North America's first Jewish congregation, Shearith Israel, in 1654. In years to come, people of other faiths brought new forms of worship. "Mother" Ann Lee established the first U.S. Shaker community in Watervliet. Joseph Smith reported an angelic visit, published *The Book of Mormon* in Palmyra, and founded the Church of Jesus Christ of Latter-day

Whosoever Reports a Thing by Harry Lieberman, c. 1976. Born to a Hasidic Jewish sect in Poland, he began painting at age 80. Many of his works illustrate Jewish folklore and literature—here, the story of Queen Esther. *Museum of American Folk Art Below:* St. Patrick's Day Parade passes St. Patrick's Cathedral on Fifth Avenue. Designed by James Renwick and completed in 1859, the building testifies to growing Irish influence in 19th-century New York. *Photo Dan Budnik*

Saints in Fayette. The 20th century's genocidal wars sent waves of exiles to New York, where they enriched American life and arts—among them songwriters Irving Berlin and Kurt Weill. In the 1990s, war in Bosnia brought a community of Muslims to Utica, adding yet another voice to the eclectic chorus of New York prayers. ♦

"WE HAVE HERE PAPISTS, MENNONITES, AND LUTHERANS among the Dutch, also many Puritans or Independents and many atheists and various other servants of Baal.... It would create still greater confusion, if the obstinate and immovable Jews came to settle here."

Governor Peter Stuyvesant, 1654

On the Erie Canal

In a flash of glory that lasted but 30 years, the Erie Canal brought New York fame and fortune. A Geneva farmer suggested that a canal could open inland trade by linking the Hudson to the Great Lakes. Many were skeptical, but De Witt Clinton won the governor's office in 1817 by supporting the project, later dubbed "Clinton's Ditch." Opening day in 1825 brought fireworks and odes as the governor carried a keg of Lake Erie water from Buffalo to New York Harbor. The cost of moving a ton of Midwest freight to harbor dropped from $100 to $6; ships crowded the Hudson en route to ports at Buffalo, Rochester, and Albany.

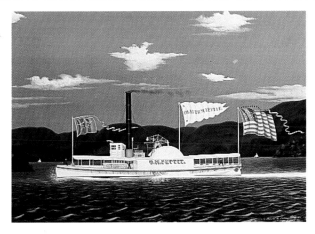

The Oliver M. Pettit by James Bard, 1857. New Yorkers today are rediscovering the pleasures of river travel, after a century of trains, planes, and automobiles. *America Hurrah Archive, New York.* Opposite above: Portrait of De Witt Clinton, attributed to Samuel Lovett Waldo, c. 1884. Governor Clinton won an incredible 95 percent of the popular vote by promising to build the Erie Canal. *Museum of the City of New York.* Opposite below: *Erie Canal, New York* by John William Hill, 1832. A boisterous canal culture took hold along the Erie, with "canawlers" serenading their mules, skiffs and steamboats racing to the ocean and back, and frontier outposts enjoying boom times. *New-York Historical Society*

Towns along the Erie grew prosperous while others scrambled to join the action by building feeder canals. By the 1850s, the railroad took over the region's commerce, and many Erie boomtowns slipped into neglect. The final blow came in the 1950s with the opening of the St. Lawrence Seaway.

Drop a tear for big-foot Sal,
The best damn cook on the Erie Canal.
She aimed for Heaven but she went to Hell—
Fifteen years on the Erie Canal....
There weren't no bar where she hadn't been,
    From Albany to Buffalo.

One of many earthy songs of the Erie "canawlers," rough-and-ready boatmen who hauled freight on mule-drawn barges

Above: Clinton Square, 1871 or *Syracuse by Moonlight* by Johann M. Culverhouse, 1871. *Onondaga Historical Association. Below:* Model of a New York Central locomotive, 1949. *Photo Model Railroader Magazine*

New York by Rail

Railroads arrived in New York in 1831 in the form of a 16-mile line from Schenectady to Albany, cutting off a curve in the Erie Canal. A year later, the line was extended west to Saratoga, and Schenectady became the first U.S. railroad terminus. By the early 1840s, eight different lines led from Albany to Buffalo, a 25-hour trip, barring delays. The railroads found their champion in Cornelius "Commodore" Vanderbilt, who bought up various lines to create the New York Central Railroad. Terminal cities from New York to Buffalo erected grand station houses for their patron company.

New York Underground

New York City's subway gets a bum rap. Its graffiti provoked worldwide censure before the trains were stainproofed in the 1980s and "underground" artists like Keith Haring graduated to downtown galleries. Rumors of crime have kept tourists away, but recent improvements have made it more likely to encounter a pianist than a pickpocket. New York City's compressed masses—3.5 million each day—travel one of the world's great underground systems, with 700 miles of track. Earlier in this century, they jostled above-ground along the clattering curves of the "el." Underground tunnels slowly took over, despite rivers, bedrock, and turns that taxed engineering know-how. By the time the city assumed operation, a majority of New Yorkers used the subway to get to work, the beach, three major league baseball stadiums, and two world's fairs.

Untitled (subway drawing) by Keith Haring, 1983. The late pop artist was one of many *graffitisti* to ply his trade on city-supplied "canvases." *Estate of Keith Haring* Left: *Seventh Avenue Subway* by James W. Kerr, 1931. *Museum of the City of New York*

The Rail Road Suspension Bridge: Near Niagara Falls by Charles Parsons for Currier & Ives, 1856. Completed in 1855, the iron bridge with its Egyptian Revival columns supported heavy locomotive traffic with the new trick of suspension. *Museum of the City of New York Below: My Dog Spot* (painted hard hat) by Richard Glazer-Danay (Mohawk), 1982. Starting in 1886, Mohawks have helped raise New York's steel skyline of bridges and skyscrapers. *American Indian Contemporary Arts, San Francisco*

No engineering marvel won greater admiration from New Yorkers—and the nation—than the web of bridges that unfurled across the 19th-century sky. Even at Niagara, tourists turned from the roaring cataract to have a snapshot taken against John Roebling's Niagara Railway Suspension Bridge, situated just downriver. The bridge's success made an important aesthetic point: human interaction could improve a landscape. German-born Roebling went on to fame and tragedy when he designed a "Brooklyn Bridge" to span the East River, linking Manhattan and Brooklyn (he died early in the project after slipping on a piling, and his daughter-in-law, Emily Warren Roebling, oversaw the last decade of work). Roebling revolutionized bridge engineering by strengthening iron cable with parallel strands of steel.

He also stretched the public's idea of architectural beauty by allowing his arcing lines of support to create the dominant visual effect. Every New Yorker has a favorite bridge—Rip Van Winkle or Tappan Zee, Bear Mountain or the Verrazano. For songwriter Paul Simon, the modest 59th Street Bridge was reason enough for "Feelin' Groovy." But artists have devoted a disproportionate share of words, paint, and music to the many-stranded magic of the Brooklyn Bridge. ●

O harp and altar, of the fury fused,
(How could mere toil align thy
    choiring strings!)
Terrific threshold of the prophet's pledge,
Prayer of pariah, and the lover's cry,—
...Through the bound cable strands,
    the arching path
Upward, veering with light, the flight
    of strings,—
Taut miles of shuttling moonlight
    syncopate
The whispered rush, telepathy
    of wires....

Hart Crane, from "To Brooklyn Bridge," 1930

The Brooklyn Bridge: Variation on an Old Theme by Joseph Stella, 1939. Stella brought Cubism from Europe to celebrate an icon of his adopted town in a series of paintings.

The French architect Le Corbusier preferred Cass Gilbert's creation, the George Washington Bridge over the Hudson. *Whitney Museum of American Art, New York*

Skating in Central Park by Agnes Tait, 1934. A lifeline to generations of New Yorkers, Central Park offers seasonal pleasures and unexpected paths, ponds, and bridges. National Museum of American Art/Art Resource

Art of the Park

With great social optimism, New York planners have coaxed both art and nature into spaces for communal play and refuge. In 1857 Frederick Law Olmsted and Calvert Vaux won a competition to design a "central park" for New York City. They proposed lawns, forests, a lake, and twisting country paths—elements long lost from the city—and created an oasis to delight generations of New Yorkers. For urban relief upstate, Governor Nelson Rockefeller in the 1960s commissioned painting and sculpture from modern masters working throughout the state—including natives Mary Callery, Allan

D'Arcangelo, and Helen Frankenthaler, as well as outlanders Louise Nevelson, Claes Oldenburg, and Mark Rothko—lightening the stark geometry of the civic center at Albany Mall. Besides improving on nature, New Yorkers have respected its original splendor by preserving Adirondack State Park and the glacier's masterpiece, Niagara Falls. Perhaps the finest marriage of art and

nature can be found at the Storm King Art Center in Cornwall-on-Hudson, where the soaring sculptures of Richard Serra, David Smith, Henry Moore, Louise Bourgeois, and other postwar masters offer dramatic counterpoint to their backdrop, the Shawangunk Mountains and the Hudson River Valley.

"THE PARK IS INTENDED TO FURNISH HEALTHFUL recreation for the poor and the rich, the young and the old, the vicious and the virtuous, so far as each can partake therein without infringing upon the rights of others.... The final artistic effect will be much finer than could possibly be obtained upon a tract of the richest and most easily worked soil, the natural outlines of which were tame and prosaic."

Frederick Law Olmsted, "Description of Central Park," 1859

Left: Voltron XX by David Smith, 1963. *Storm King Art Center.* **Above: Central Park Boathouse, c. 1880. Designers Frederick Law Olmsted and** **Calvert Vaux hoped their project would unite city residents in restorative leisure.** *Museum of the City of New York. Photo August Hepp*

Great Expositions

America's Utopian hopes found realization in New York's great fairs. Buffalo hosted a Pan-American Exhibit in 1901, eager to display its new railroad- and steel-based wealth. Porticoed temples and scientific inventions covered 350 acres. A generation later, the 1939 World's Fair came to Flushing Meadows, Queens. The fair committee chased Depression-era blues with Gershwin melodies (some written for the fair) and with their model "city of tomorrow." Exhibits from dozens of countries suggested idealized communities across a cooperating world—a fantastic vision for 1939, with a new war brewing. The World's Fair returned to Flushing Meadows

The New York World's Fair by Alice Mumford Culin, 1937. The Trylon and Perisphere were high modernist icons of the 1939 fair. Designers Harrison and Fouilhoux drew on the ideas of Henri Matisse, who posited that all forms could be resolved into triangle, sphere, or cube. *Library of Congress*

Guiding Spirit or Despot?

New York City Parks Commissioner Robert Moses (1889–1981) reigned over the city's public works for half a century, planning highways, bridges, parks, beaches, public housing, and two world's fairs. After winning raves for opening Long Island's beachfront with parks and parkways, Moses focused increasingly on the automobile. His web of highways created a city of cars, enduring traffic woes, and brave pedestrians.

in 1964, offering a window on the space age and a forum for the works of Pop artists Roy Lichtenstein, Robert Rauschenberg, and Andy Warhol.

"IN THE DARKEST DAYS OF THE DEPRESsion, they dreamed of orderly hygienic cities and houses....They looked ahead to safe, fast travel on luxurious streamlined aircraft, trains, buses, ships, and automobiles. Unlike modern architects, whose utopias rarely develop beyond the drawing stage, the first American industrial designers were able to build their model city, the 1939 New York World's Fair."

Donald Bush, The Streamlined Decade, *1975*

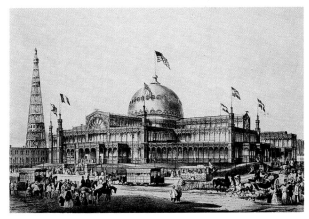

Above: **The 1964 World's Fair, with its signature Unisphere, rises in Queens. Futuristic artifacts from the 1964 fair—the Unisphere and three saucer-capped towers—survive to intrigue present-day viewers, and even provided a plot twist for the pop sci-fi film** *Men in Black.* **Photo The New York Times.** *Left:* **America's first World's Fair came to New York's Crystal Palace in 1853. Currier & Ives engraving.** *Museum of the City of New York*

Riot at Union Square, March 6, 1930 by Peter Hopkins, 1947. *Museum of the City of New York* Union Square was a meeting place for the jobless during the Depression. Unemployed workers and leftist sympathizers clashed violently with police on this date.

The tangle of New York's politics tends to pit the metropolis against the rest of the state, as the city—so populous, so liberal, so expensive to run—claims a big share of tax dollars from upstate Albany, conservative and national in outlook. The two power centers breed different sorts of politicians. Albany statespeople like to keep an eye on that other capitol in Washington. Some New York governors won fame by never running for national office (Mario Cuomo) or by never winning (Thomas E. Dewey

TWO GREAT QUESTIONS.   *Th. Nast*

WHO STOLE THE PEOPLE'S MONEY? — DO TELL . NY.TIMES   'TWAS HIM.

Who Stole the People's Money? **This cartoon by Thomas Nast from an 1871** *Harper's Weekly* **depicts figures from the Tammany Hall scandal passing the blame. "Boss" Tweed is pictured on the left.** *New-York Historical Society Below:* **Pipe with carvings of New York natives Franklin and Eleanor (on reverse side) Roosevelt. Artist unknown, n.d.** *Franklin D. Roosevelt Library.* **Photo Henry Groskinsky**

and Nelson Rockefeller). But both Franklin Delano Roosevelt and his cousin, Theodore, made the leap from Albany to the White House. "T. R." in fact began his political life as a New York City police commissioner, where he fought remnants of the corrupt Tammany Hall machine. Tammany ruled late 19th century New York, buying votes, plundering budgets, and supporting chosen immigrants through "honest graft." Its bribery-based regime cost the city an estimated $200 million— in 19th-century dollars! ♠

Politics as Show Business

Today New York politics still means pleasing diverse immigrants, though bullying has given way to sarcastic native humor. Consequently, New York City mayors perform better on late night comedy shows than in national polls. Ed Koch—a Johnny Carson regular—started the trend. Mayoral candidates such as Bella Abzug, Norman Mailer, and Al Sharpton have raised politics to performance art. Even Republican Rudolph Giuliani has done his turn—in drag—on *Saturday Night Live*. As for recent national bids, Geraldine Ferraro made history as the first woman to run for vice president on a major ticket.

First Feminists

In 1848, Elizabeth Cady Stanton, Lucretia Mott, and 100 other respectable women gathered in Seneca Falls, where Stanton read aloud the "Declaration of Sentiments and Resolutions": "We hold these truths to be self-evident, that all men *and women* are created equal." The movement for women's vote spread across the country, and two generations later, actresses Ethel Barrymore, Mary Shaw, and Lillian Russell led a 1908 parade of suffragists down Fifth Avenue. Someone upstate got the message, and in 1917, New York granted women the vote. It took a few more generations before New Yorkers such as Eleanor Roosevelt, Geraldine Ferraro, and Gloria Steinem rose to prominence.

"IT IS STARTLING TO REALIZE THAT ONE IS SO DEEPLY, fanatically disliked by a number of people. And yet, while I weigh as honestly as I can their grounds for disapproval, when I feel that I am right in what I do, it seems to me that I cannot afford, as a self-respecting individual, to refuse to do a thing merely because it will make me disliked or bring down a storm of criticism on my head."

Eleanor Roosevelt, The Autobiography of Eleanor Roosevelt, *1958*
Born in New York City in 1884, Roosevelt served as the state's
first lady, the nation's first lady, and then returned in 1945 to
serve as U.S. delegate to the United Nations.

Above: Former New York City Mayor Ed Koch on his radio show. Koch's famous line as mayor was "How'm I doin'?" He put New York wit to work with signs such as "Don't even *think* of parking here." *Photo Don Hogan Charles/The New York Times Right: Por Los Niños* by Alfredo Hernández, 1976. This mural on P.S. 97 on Houston Street was painted by junior high school students directed by Hernández. *Opposite above:* Elizabeth Cady Stanton by Anna Klumpke, 1889. *National Portrait Gallery/Art Resource Opposite below:* The late Bella Abzug, who represented New York in Congress for many years, is remembered for her forthright speech, fabulous hats, and fearless advocacy for progressive causes. *Photo Monica Almeida/The New York Times*

The Lyndhurst Estate in Tarrytown. Considered the finest surviving Gothic Revival house in the country, this marble edifice was built in 1838 and extensively enlarged in 1865. Its features include multiple parapets, castellations, foil windows, and grouped chimneys; the interiors are equally elaborate. *Photo Lee Snider. Below:* Columned porch of a 1903 Stanford White house in Sands Point, Long Island. *Photo Pieter Estersohn*

Architecture Unbound

Four centuries of eclectic influence have left a diverse legacy of New York dwellings. Early settlers built low: Dutch Colonial style hugged the ground, with stonework and slanted

roofs nestling between the windmills of Manhattan and Albany. The 20th century built high, carving living space out of skyscrapers and converted industrial warehouses. The intervening years brought a veritable survey of world architecture, notably a 19th-century wave of revival styles that competed to house New York's new wealthy. From Fifth Avenue to the banks of the Hudson, Greek porticoes vied with Egyptian obelisks, Italian Renaissance villas, French mansard roofs, and Gothic turrets. Textile tycoon C. T. Longstreet commissioned a castle replete with Gothic arches and Romanesque towers—vast enough to house Syracuse University's journalism school. Both name and unknown architects contributed to the emergence of a native style. Houses in Rochester and Saratoga Springs sported fanciful Victorian porches and Arts and Crafts–inspired trellises. Long Island boasts a generous share of classically elegant estates, as well as distinguished experiments in machine-age design that admit ocean and sky through glass walls, skylights, and expansive decks.

Above: A converted townhouse in Manhattan's Greenwich Village features waxed glass windows and floors made of high-tech aeronautical material. *Photo Pieter Estersohn. Left:* Contemporary home in East Hampton, Long Island, designed by Alastair Standing. *Photo Scott Frances*

"Beauty rests on utility."

Shaker saying

Shaker Style and Adirondack Rustic

One of the first genuine American aesthetics arose among the Shakers of New York. "Mother" Ann Lee left Liverpool in 1774, leading eight followers to the upstate village of Watervliet, where she founded the first Shaker community in America. Shaker philosophy took much from Quakerism: members shared all worldly goods and emphasized communal harmony. They danced to "shake" off evil, for which their meetinghouses opened to a central dance space. All of Shaker design supported a belief in simplicity, harmony, and order. In a time when most settlers valued acquisition and display, Shakers rejected ornament and focused on the clean lines of utility.

Among the most successful American sects, the Shakers are mostly gone now, but their aesthetic lives on in serene harmony with modern design—indeed, with almost any interior style.

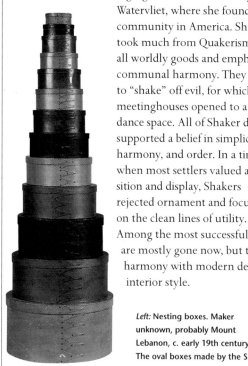

Left: Nesting boxes. Maker unknown, probably Mount Lebanon, c. early 19th century. The oval boxes made by the Shakers in graduated sizes showed very fine workmanship and finishes. *America Hurrah Archive, New York Photo David Schorsch Collection*

In the late 19th century a few pioneers sensed design potential in the gnarled trees of the Adirondack back-country, and wealthy city dwellers began to mimic the rustic style in their vacation homes. Adirondack "great camps" appeared between the Civil War and World War II, some growing into mansions and sprawling resorts with playful names like Kamp Kill Kare, Pine Knot, and Paowync (an acronym for the names of railroad stocks). Local style favored resourcefulness and one-of-a-kind creations, following the craft ethic advanced by Gustav Stickley. Local craftsmen fashioned tables and chairs out of yellow birch, applied fanciful detail in white birch bark, and bent cedar into elaborate twig mosaics and aromatic sideboards. Their legacy survives in the slat-backed Adirondack chair, a lawn perennial.

Above: Bay window with applied bark and twig trim at Camp Pine Knot, c. 1895. *Photo Craig Gilborn. Left:* The master bedroom at Kamp Kill Kare, c. 1900. Photographer unknown. City visitors imported opulence but emulated native style. *Adirondack Museum*

All That Glitters: New York's Gilded Age

Born to wealth in New York City in 1862, Edith Wharton 60 years later wrote a Pulitzer Prize–winning novel about her tribe and its strict social codes. The clan's leaders had amassed fortunes in railroads (Morgan, Gould, Vanderbilt), oil (Rockefeller), and mining (Guggenheim). With a bit of aesthetic guidance, they alchemized these sooty concerns into proclamations of refinement. Their architects designed city mansions and country retreats, while furniture-makers practiced the new art of "interior decoration." Wharton herself took a hand in guiding the tribe's taste: in her first published book, *The Decoration of Houses,* she and her architect coauthor offered such helpful hints to millionaires as: "It is obvious that the banqueting-hall should be less brilliant than a ball-room and less fanciful in decoration than a music room." The phrase "the Gilded Age" hails from that genius of the common man, Mark Twain.

"A VISIT TO MRS. MANSON MINGOTT WAS ALWAYS AN amusing episode to the young man. The house in itself was already an historic document, though not, of course, as venerable as certain other old family houses in University Place and lower Fifth Avenue. Those were of the purest 1830… whereas old Mrs. Mingott…had bodily cast out the massive furniture of her prime, and mingled with the Mingott heirlooms the frivolous upholstery of the Second Empire."

Edith Wharton, The Age of Innocence, *1920*

Above: Flower-form Vase by Louis Comfort Tiffany, c. 1917. *Metropolitan Museum of Art. Left:* Bedroom of the John D. Rockefeller residence, 1884–1937. *Museum of the City of New York. Opposite above: The Terrace Bridge, Central Park* by Maurice Prendergast, 1901. *Art Institute of Chicago. Opposite below: Edith Wharton* by Edward Harrison May, 1870. *National Portrait Gallery/Art Resource*

Washington Irving acquired his Tarrytown farmhouse, Sunnyside, in 1835 and remodeled it extensively, adding gables, dormers, and towers until it was "as full of angles and corners as an old cocked hat." The 17-room fairytale home, with its landscaped gardens and ponds, is open to the public; it contains some of Irving's furniture and many of his books.
Photo Scott Barrow

Great Estates

For the wealthy who craved a patch of earth, New York's Hudson Valley offered the proper setting for a country estate. Rolling hills and granite bluffs afforded views worthy of great landscaping, and easy access to Manhattan and Albany. The homes and gardens of Dutchess, Putnam, and Columbia Counties showcase period styles ranging from the whimsical Dutch farmhouse of Washington Irving's Sunnyside to the beaux-arts grandeur of Kykuit, the Rockefeller estate to which Nelson Rockefeller added dramatic 20th-century sculpture. Farther upriver sits the state's best example of Federal style, Boscobel;

Olana

After establishing himself as one of America's foremost landscape painters, Frederic Church bought land overlooking the Hudson River he so often painted. Olana, the Persian-style castle he and his wife built, incorporated Indian, Chinese, Mexican, Italian, Gothic, and other exotic details. They took landscaping no less seriously, consulting Calvert Vaux and planting thousands of trees and creating a lake to mirror the land and sky. As Church understood, Olana's crowning glory was its view: you could see 60 miles south to West Point, and more than 35 north, past Albany. Olana is enjoying new fame as a museum that recaptures the look of 1891, the year the estate was completed.

several Roosevelt estates including FDR's Hyde Park; and Olana, masterpiece of its doting creator, Frederic Church. Many of these owe their survival to local efforts to protect and restore them—testifying to pride of place and the belief that such beauty, even if designed for the few, should be enjoyed by the many.

Above: Olana from the Southwest by Frederic Church, c. 1872. *Cooper-Hewitt, National Design Museum, Smithsonian Institution. Opposite below:* Rose trellis in the French gardens designed for Helena Woolworth McCann (daughter of the dime-store founder) by Annette Hoyt Flanders in Oyster Bay, Long Island, 1927. *Smithsonian Institution*

Steeplechase Park, Coney Island by Leo McKay, 1898. *Museum of the City of New York.* Steeplechase Park opened in 1897, one of three enclosed attractions that defined Coney Island. Designer George C. Tilyou filled 15 acres with spinning rides and practical jokes, offering crowds comic relief from city formality. The park took its name from the mechanical steeplechase horses that raced around its rim. *Below:* Nathan's hot dog stand at Coney Island. *Photo The New York Times*

High Life and Hot Dogs

Around the turn of the century, Coney Island came into its own. Earlier the park had catered to the wealthy and the footloose, who took a six-mile ferry trip to the narrow stretch of beach on Brooklyn's south shore. But with the elevated railway in the 1880s came the working millions. Off went Victorian bustles; in came bathing suits. Carnival rides, freak shows, fortune tellers, even ladies of questionable virtue lined the beach, greeting millions of visitors each summer weekend. Notes historian David Ellis, "Where else could you have a vacation for a nickel!" Coney Island's famous parachute jump and Steeplechase Park are fond memories, but the region has found new life as "Little Odessa," a haven for Russian immigrants.

Saratoga Society

In the years after the Civil War, Saratoga Springs rivaled Newport as a summer haven for the likes of Vanderbilts, Morgans, and Whitneys. Some "took the waters" in natural springs first used by the Mohawks. Others took in the famed horse races, and the racing crowd still repairs here in August when metropolitan tracks close. Creativity took center stage with the 1960s opening of the Saratoga Performing Arts Center, summer home to the New York City Ballet, the Philadelphia Orchestra, and noted jazz festivals. Yaddo, a retreat founded by the Trask family in 1926, offers gracious seclusion to the artistic elite.

Saratoga in Racing Season by Guy Pene du Bois, 1937. In this mural in Saratoga's post office, well-heeled fans watch race horses parade to the starting line. *Left:* On the course at Saratoga during racing season. The nation's oldest racecourse, it has hosted meets since 1863. *Photo Scott Barrow*

Built in 1923 to accommodate swelling crowds, Yankee Stadium was renovated in the 1970s, but "the house that Ruth built" faces an uncertain future. *Photo Jake Rajs/Tony Stone Images. Opposite:* Dodger die-hards, 1949; one wears a button urging his team to "Moider dem Yanks." *UPI/Corbis. Opposite below:* Jackie Robinson's famous steal of home plate helped the Dodgers beat the Yankees in the 1955 World Series. *Photo Meyer Liebowitz/The New York Times*

Bombers and Bums

Nowhere is baseball more important than in New York, where teams inspire tribal bonds, earn ticker-tape parades, and break hearts in about equal measure. Glory days began in 1923, when Babe Ruth christened a new Bronx ballpark with the Yankees' first World Series victory. Lou Gehrig soon joined the lineup, which in 1927 became infamous as "murderers' row." The Bombers won 17 championships in 34 years (1923–56). Across the river in Manhattan, a young Willie Mays cut his teeth with the Giants at the Polo Grounds. And in Brooklyn, local pride surged around the Dodgers, who broke the color line by signing Jackie Robinson in 1947 and made it to eight World Series, only to fall to the Yankees in six of them. Brooklyn still mourns the 1958 departure of the Bums for L.A.—the very year that the Giants left for San Francisco. Many local images are preserved at the sport's pantheon, the Baseball Hall of Fame, in Cooperstown. The upstate museum displays everything from Bobby Thompson's bat (his homer clinched the pennant for the '51 Giants) to the ball that won the '86 Series for the Mets—upstart newcomers whose logo unites Dodger blue and Giant orange.

"NATURALLY, ALL THE GOOD PEOPLE WERE Dodger fans. If a guy was a Yankee fan, you knew he was a nerd, out of touch. He was probably anti-union, not for good causes, had a rich uncle somewhere. If someone was a Giant fan, he was mixed up, like an anarchist, a nihilist—he was doing it to spite his family....Dodger fans were the salt of the earth...."

Joel Berger, in It Happened in Brooklyn, *1993*

The Baseball Hall of Fame

As far as anyone can tell, the first baseball game was played in 1839, when Abner Doubleday drew a diamond field in a Cooperstown park. The central New York town founded by the father of James Fenimore Cooper now houses the National Baseball Hall of Fame. Only 1 percent of all players are voted in by the Baseball Writers Association. The museum covers the Negro League, women's leagues, and other chapters in America's old-time pastime.

Dorothy Parker and Robert Benchley, at right, pose with their employers in 1919; from left: *Vanity Fair* editor Frank Crowninshield, *Vogue* editor Edna Chase, and publisher Condé Nast. Parker, Benchley, and their cronies made up the famous Round Table at Manhattan's Algonquin Hotel in the 1920s. Photograph by Robert Sherwood. *Courtesy Boston University Libraries. Below: Edna St. Vincent Millay by Charles Ellis, 1934. National Portrait Gallery/Art Resource*

New York looms large in the dreams of literary and performing artists, drawing a critical mass of talent. Actors aspire to Broadway footlights. Musicians hear cheers at Carnegie Hall, the Apollo, Birdland. Dancers leap across the stages of Lincoln Center or Radio City Music Hall. Writers see a fat envelope, check enclosed. Ever since P. T. Barnum invited Jenny Lind to sing at the Castle Garden Theater in 1850, a New York debut has meant arrival on the world's stage. And for artists-in-training, the state offers some of the finest conservatories, studios, and workshops on the planet. ●

Literary New York

The latest trend in Manhattan nightlife might shock a few English teachers. Every week young literary lights compete in a downtown "poetry slam" before cheering crowds. But language has long been blood sport in these parts. A century ago, Danish immigrant Jacob Riis wrote candid descriptions of tenement squalor in *How the Other Half Lives,* inspiring new laws as well as fellow muckrakers Lincoln Steffens and Ida Tarbell. William Dean Howells turned the journalistic impulse to realist fiction and defended novelists Stephen Crane and Theodore Dreiser when their accounts of prostitution outraged moral watchdogs.

Then as now, New York offered writers a mix of gritty material and kindred neighbors. In Greenwich Village, John

John Reed, c. 1915. Reed's eyewitness account of the Russian Revolution, *Ten Days That Shook the World,* also shook up America's literary circles. *Photo Library of Congress/ Corbis. Left: Ichabod Crane by Norman Rockwell, 1937. Rockwell was commissioned to create illustrations for a new edition of Washington Irving's The Legend of Sleepy Hollow. Draper Visual Arts and the Norman Rockwell Family Trust*

Reed explored Marxism, Eugene O'Neill tested plays, and Edna St. Vincent Millay revived the sonnet—many of them meeting at Mabel Dodge's salon. Uptown, Jessie Fauset and A'Lelia Walker hosted soirees for leaders of the Harlem Renaissance. Others have taken the lighter side, like Dorothy Parker and her witty comrades at the Algonquin Round Table; and Mark Twain, declaring that he wanted to live up to

the title "Belle of New York" during his long sojourns.

The best of New York's literature has had wide appeal. Washington Irving's *The Legend of Sleepy Hollow* spoke to Europe in the voice of a new land; James Fenimore Cooper's Leather-

stocking tales went west with real-life pioneers. But if New York writers aim for the world, they also look homeward. Walt Whitman sang for America but exulted for his native Long Island and adopted Brooklyn. William Kennedy brought Albany to Hollywood's big screen with *Ironweed. Underworld* takes Don DeLillo back to the Bronx; *Now and Then* finds young Joseph Heller in Coney Island. And some neighborhoods enjoy ongoing literary renewal: the Lower East Side of Philip Roth and E. L. Doctorow is now the *loisida* of strong young voices speaking in Latin rhythms.

"OF ALL THE AMBITIONS OF THE great unpublished, the one that is strongest, the most abiding, is the ambition to get to New York. For these, New York is the *point de départ,* the pedestal, the niche, the indispensable vantage ground."

Frank Norris

"NEW YORK [IN 1919] HAD ALL THE iridescence of the beginning of the world. The returning troops marched up Fifth Avenue...and there was gala in the air. As I hovered ghost-like in the Plaza Red Room of a Sunday afternoon, or went to lush and liquid garden parties in the East Sixties or tippled with Princetonians in the Biltmore Bar, I was haunted always by my other life—my drab room in the Bronx...my shabby suits, my poverty, and love.... I was a failure—mediocre at advertising work and unable to get started as a writer."

F. Scott Fitzgerald, "My Lost City," 1932

Left: **John Cheever** by Henry Koerner, 1964 *Time* magazine cover. Cheever was the bard of the New York sub-urbs. *Time, Inc./Art Resource.* **Below:** Norman Mailer with fellow nov-elist Joyce Carol Oates at the PEN Congress in 1986. Mailer, a Brooklyn native, has said that the borough is the only "particular place I think of as home." *Photo Robert McElroy*

We were very tired,
    we were very merry—
We had gone back and forth
    all night on the ferry...

*Edna St. Vincent Millay,
in "Recuerdo," 1920*

Chinese Theater by Howard McClean, 1905. *Museum of the City of New York. Below:* Poster advertising matinee idol John Barrymore in a 1922 production of *Hamlet.* Drawing by E. Cadmus. *Performing Arts Research Center/ New York Public Library Opposite above:* The musical *Hair* rocked Broadway in 1967. *Photo Dagmar. Opposite below:* Barbra Streisand in *Funny Girl,* drawing by Al Hirschfeld, 1975. *Margo Feiden Galleries, New York*

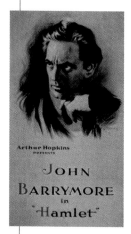

Behind the Footlights

Been to Times Square lately? New York's theater district has hawked peep-show thrills and high-minded drama—often in the same show—for over a century. Oscar Hammerstein I opened the first theater in 1895, selling 4,000 more tickets than he had seats and creating a stampede. Ziegfeld and his Follies kept the mood light and the legs flashing through the 1920s. Slowly, serious actors drew the spotlight, including the Barrymore clan, Paul Robeson, and Marlon Brando—a product of Lee Strasberg's Actors Studio, which still trains stars from Robert De Niro to Claire Danes. In 1920 a young man born on 43d Street, Eugene O'Neill, ushered in the age of the playwright by winning the Pulitzer Prize for *Beyond the Horizon;* in his wake came native talents Neil Simon and Wendy Wasserstein and the best dramatists from across the land.

The theater district pushed uptown to Lincoln Center and downtown to Off- and Off-Off-Broadway and Joseph Papp's Public Theater. All along, Broadway kept America singing the tunes of the Gershwins, Rodgers and Hammerstein (or Hart), Frank Loesser, and Stephen Sondheim. For decades its glamour contrasted starkly with dingy streets and dubious storefronts—but new corporate money is sprucing up the sidewalks and renovating the old, echoing houses.

Laughter in the Hills

Each summer between 1920 and 1970, close to a million New York Jews escaped the city swelter for the Catskill Mountains. Swank resorts like Grossinger's and the Concord offered family entertainment—shuffleboard and lake swims—by day and comedy by night. "Borscht Belt" humor drew on Yiddish theater to launch the careers of comics like Jackie Mason, Mel Brooks, Alan King, even Howard Stern. By the 1980s, the comedy scene had shifted back to town, but the Catskills never lost their natural charms—and the resorts may be headed for a revival.

New York on Film

King Kong swatting airplanes atop the Empire State Building. Woody Allen and Diane Keaton taking in dawn and the Brooklyn Bridge to the strains of Gershwin. Brooklyn's summer swelter in Spike Lee's *Do the Right Thing*—New York has provided icons of the movie age. Less well-known is the state's role in growing the industry: in the 1920s more than 100 films were made in Astoria, Queens, where pioneers developed the new movie technology. In the age of the "talkie," Astoria studios engineered the Marx Brothers's move from Broadway to the screen—and Paramount's dramatic newsreels. Film crews still descend on the state in locations ranging from midtown to millionaire's retreat, and TV heroes Bill Cosby and Big Bird can take the 59th Street Bridge to the studios with the skyline view.

Left: Chorus girls take a break in the dressing room between scenes during the 1928 filming of *Broadway. Hulton Getty Collection/Tony Stone Images. Above:* Poster for the movie *King Kong*, with its beleaguered star atop the Empire State Building. *Photofest Opposite above:* Audrey Hepburn made being young and poor in New York look glamorous in *Breakfast at Tiffany's. Opposite:* Danny Aiello and Spike Lee in a scene from Lee's *Do the Right Thing.* Both, *Photofest*

"'CHAPTER ONE. HE ADORED NEW YORK CITY. HE idolized it out of all proportion.' Uh, no, make that: 'He romanticized it out of all proportion....He thrived on the hustle-bustle of the crowds and the traffic. To him, New York meant beautiful women

and street smart guys who seemed to know all the angles....' Nah, no.... I mean, let me try to be more profound....'He was as tough and romantic as the city he loved.'"

Woody Allen's character, in voice-over,
Manhattan, 1979

A New York Filmography

A Night at the Opera Marx Brothers madness

King Kong Fay Wray and the big ape atop the Empire State Building

Ragtime Passion and politics in old New York

Crossing Delancey Second-generation Jews on the Lower East Side

The Great Gatsby High society meets low society on Long Island

Taxi Driver Scorsese character study

Annie Hall Woody Allen and Diane Keaton take Manhattan, to the strains of Gershwin

Ironweed Gritty look at the wrong side of Albany's tracks

The Taking of Pelham 123 Manhattan's subway system held hostage

Nobody's Fool Paul Newman finds hope in wintry Poughkeepsie

Breakfast at Tiffany's Forever Audrey...

The Age of Innocence Gilded Age glamour and intrigue

Moonstruck Nicolas Cage woos Cher with hearts and flour

Wall Street When masters of the universe collide

Do the Right Thing Spike Lee and friends in Brooklyn's summer swelter

Right: Tap pioneer Bill "Bojangles" Robinson in 1928. *Beinecke Library, Yale University. Below:* In 1933 Rochester native Lincoln Kirstein invited George Balanchine of Diaghilev's Ballets Russes to establish America's first school of classical ballet and the New York City Ballet. Here, company principals Heather Watts and Sean Lavery with the corps de ballet in a 1983 performance of Balanchine's *Concerto Barocco.* *Photo Martha Swope*

Soft Shoe to Toe Shoes

New Yorkers have tried new dance steps since at least 1767, when whites donned blackface to mimic slave dances. In 1911 Al Jolson dazzled New York with his own song and dance, and the town began to welcome authentic imports. Bill "Bojangles" Robinson brought his "soft shoe" routine to vaudeville, where it met European clog dancing to become tap. George Balanchine's New York City Ballet took the stage in 1948. Martha Graham made her New York and world debuts in 1926, and modern dance still draws on her legacy. Alvin Ailey, Robert Joffrey, and Merce Cunningham created companies that explore diverse contemporary or ethnic themes, while social

dancers explored African and Latin rhythms. Jazz dance found its way to Broadway when Balanchine collaborated with tap star Herbie Harper in *Slaughter on Tenth Avenue.* By the time *Cabaret* and *Hair* won Broadway and movie kudos, Bob Fosse and Twyla Tharp had established the choreographer as a linchpin in stage success.

The bookless musical *Dancin'* was directed and choreographed by Bob Fosse, who also choreographed *The Pajama Game, Pippin,* and *Cabaret.* His edgy style set the tone for contemporary theatrical dance. *Photo Martha Swope/Time, Inc.* Below: Alvin Ailey's company performs the choreographer's *Night Creature. Alvin Ailey American Dance Theater and Dance Theater Foundation, Inc. Photo Barbara Bordnick*

"THE BALLET THAT WAS OUTLINED BY Oscar Hammerstein [for *Oklahoma!*] was a circus. And I was the one who said it didn't make any sense. Oscar said, 'You've got to have a light ballet to end act one with, you can't send them out into the lobby with gloom.' I said, 'Why not? Just depress the hell out of them.' And then I did my spiel and they listened…because they were very gifted men. But I absolutely threw out that first ballet."

Choreographer Agnes de Mille, on the collaboration that led to her classic "dream ballet" for Rodgers and Hammerstein's Oklahoma!

George Gershwin at the Piano by William Auerbach-Levy, 1926. The Brooklyn-born composer scored his first hit with "Swanee," recorded by Al Jolson. The musicals he wrote with brother Ira as lyricist graced Broadway throughout the 1920s and 30s; many of their songs are American standards. *Museum of the City of New York Below:* Metropolitan Opera stars including Kathleen Battle in the third act of Mozart's *The Marriage of Figaro,* 1985. *Photo Robert McElroy*

A Musical Mecca

From be-bop to hip-hop, New York's rhythms have inspired the century's new sounds. Among the New Yorkers to compose a distinctly American sound: Aaron Copland, whose

Appalachian Spring won a Pulitzer in 1945, and George Gershwin, whose *Rhapsody in Blue* mesmerized the 1939 World's Fair. Jazz collided with New York's energy to take on tones both "hot" and "cool." From the Depression through the postwar boom, dixieland combos jammed on 52nd Street; up in Harlem, Cab Calloway led big-band swings at

> ### "Playing 'bop' is like playing Scrabble with all the vowels missing."
>
> *Edward Kennedy "Duke" Ellington, 1954*

the Savoy. The 1940s found Thelonius Monk, Dizzy Gillespie, and Charlie "Bird" Parker playing dizzying strings of notes they called "be-bop" at Minton's Playhouse and Birdland. At NBC's mid-town studios, record producers like Phil Spector sparked trends from doo-wop to disco. Home-grown pop stars Billy Joel, Natalie Merchant, and Salt-n-Pepa jumped from local clubs to the top 40. As for classical clout, the New York Philharmonic and Metropolitan Opera crown New York's vast pyramid of orchestral, operatic, chamber, and choral performing groups. Upstate, a folk tradition nurtured by native son Pete Seeger remains strong, with such new champions as Ani DiFranco producing her own records in Buffalo and keeping alive the music's radical roots.

Above: Duke Ellington at the Hurricane Club, New York. *Photograph by Gordon Parks, 1943. Library of Congress. Right:* The Manhattan Transfer, with its smooth, forties style harmonies, emerged in the 1970s as an alternative to the dominant punk theme in popular music and continues to stretch the limits of the a capella form. © 1997 *Atlantic Records*

Jenkin's Band by Malvin Gray Johnson, 1934. Johnson was active during the heyday of the Harlem Renaissance. He sometimes emphasized his heritage by including African imagery in his paintings. *New York Public Library* Below: Langston Hughes. Photograph by Nickolas Muray. Hughes, a poet, humorist, and playwright, remains the best-known writer of the period. His sharp social commentary captured the dualities of black life in America. *International Museum of Photography*

The neighborhood north of Manhattan's 110th Street inhabits America's consciousness as haven, ghetto, wellspring. In the years after World War I, Harlem was a promised land for African Americans: there was work, a new political awareness, and an exploding arts scene. Writers and visual artists celebrated black culture and reacted passionately to racial injustice. The NAACP and editor W. E. B. DuBois published *The Crisis,* one of several journals to provide a forum for new voices like Langston Hughes, Countee Cullen, Jean Toomer, and Jamaican émigré Claude McKay. Zora

Neale Hurston drew on Caribbean folklore in her stories and novels. Painters including Aaron Douglas and Malvin Gray Johnson explored links between modernism and African forms. The Harlem Renaissance energized American arts and provided a base for a new African-American consciousness. Today there are hints of a new renaissance as creative artists explore Harlem's legacy of hope and hardship. ♦

"LET'S BARE OUR ARMS AND PLUNGE THEM DEEP through laughter, through pain, through sorrow, through hope, through disappointment, into the very depths of the soul of our people and drag forth material crude, rough, neglected. Then let's sing it, dance it, write it, paint it."

Painter Aaron Douglas to Langston Hughes

Above: Les Fétiches by Loïs Mailou Jones, 1938. Jones was associated with the Harlem Renaissance artists early in her career; later she studied and painted in Paris while on sabbatical from Howard University. She also worked in textile design. *National Museum of American Art/ Art Resource. Left: Couple in Raccoon Coats.* Photograph by James Van Der Zee, 1932. At his studio on West 135th Street, Van Der Zee took portraits of Harlem's new middle class against romantic backdrops, but he also photographed on the streets. *Collection James Van Der Zee*

New York has lent its name, its passion, and its resources to this century's innovations in the visual arts. A combination of world events and home-grown energy helped New York City edge out Paris as the world's art capital by the late 1950s, especially in the realm of abstraction. Perhaps the sheer confidence of the place emboldened artists to look inward, away from the world, and yet know exactly where they were. But even before its name became synonymous with art, a few visionaries were translating New York's wealth of stimuli into an astonishing range of images. It's all here, as Lincoln Steffens once said, where "the city is human nature posing nude." ●

Room in New York by Edward Hopper, 1932. More than any other artist, it was Hopper, writes art critic Robert Hughes, "who saw that the old frontier had moved inward and now lay within the self." *Sheldon Memorial Art Gallery, University of Nebraska, Lincoln*

Stieglitz, Steichen, and "291"

The American arts scene was quietly revolutionized when Alfred Stieglitz and Edward Steichen opened the Little Gallery of the Photo-Secession at 291 Fifth Avenue in 1906. Stieglitz displayed his photographs of the city and Lake George, direct images that challenged the staged, soft-focus photography of the time and redefined photography as fine art. As for painting, Steichen brought news from trips to France, the hub of innovation. The pair organized the first U.S. exhibits of Rodin and Matisse in 1908, and later showed the little-known Picasso. Eager to prove that important art need not come from Europe, Stieglitz encouraged American painters including John Marin; Arthur Dove, who drew inspiration from Long Island Sound and his farm in Geneva; and Georgia O'Keeffe, whom Stieglitz later married.

"ONE DAY DURING THE WINTER SEASON OF 1902–03...WITH THE trees of Madison Square all covered with snow—fresh snow— I suddenly saw the [Flatiron] building as I had never seen it before. It looked, from where I stood, as though it were moving toward me like the bow of a monster ocean-steamer— a picture of the new America that was still in the making."

Alfred Stieglitz

Flatiron Building. Photograph by Alfred Stieglitz, 1903. Museum of Modern Art, New York

Artists on WPA by Moses Soyer, 1935. Artists who worked in the WPA included Ben Shahn, Jackson Pollock, Mark Rothko, and Norman Lewis. *National Museum of American Art.* Below: *Broadway Boogie-Woogie* by Piet Mondrian, 1942–43. The Dutch painter's minimalist vision of Manhattan's pulsating Times Square became a modernist landmark. *Museum of Modern Art, New York* Opposite: *Third Avenue* by Charles Louis Goeller, 1933–34. *National Museum of American Art*

Realism and Beyond

In the 1930s, political unrest in Europe and Russia, and depression in America, brought many leading avant-garde artists to New York. President Roosevelt's Works Project Administration provided paid work to 5,000 artists, half of them New Yorkers, who captured local memory in lasting murals for train stations, courthouses, and other public buildings. Painter Ben Shahn pushed the realist style to its political limits, portraying Ellis Island immigrants, as well as Sacco and Vanzetti, with a propagandist's passion. Others, like Jackson Pollock

and Mark Rothko, resisted the demands of realism. For these painters—who would form the core of the "New York School"—inspiration arrived with European artists. The Spanish surrealist Salvador Dalí came to town in 1939 to design a pavilion for the World's Fair and shop windows for a Fifth Avenue store. Dutch painter Piet Mondrian visited in the early 1940s. Many New Yorkers saw these new views of their own land at Peggy Guggenheim's Art of This Century gallery, which opened in 1942; soon, pioneers of Abstract Expressionism had their first shows here.

The New York School

In the mid-1950s a group of brash, confident artists met at the Cedar Tavern in Greenwich Village to discuss art theory, returning to their studios to paint in markedly individual

styles. Abstract Expressionism turned the focus from realism to art and the artist. Barnett Newman reenvisioned his native New York in solid fields of color sliced by bright lines. Mark Rothko pointed to big themes—"tragedy, ecstasy, doom"—in his floating, diffuse rectangles. Jackson Pollock became a celebrity for his swirling "action paintings"; he, along with Lee Krasner, Willem de Kooning, and Robert Motherwell, established studios on Long Island, while sculptor David Smith brought his welding torch to the Adirondacks.

The Vision Market: Pop and Op

The bustling art scene surrounding the New York School meant visibility—even celebrity—for a few working artists. Some, like sculptor Louise Nevelson, shunned the limelight. But a new generation turned further outward to embrace pop culture: if art was a commodity, why not test its limits? Roy Lichtenstein turned comic books and their grainy Ben Day dots into museum-quality paintings, blurring the line between artist and machine. Claes Oldenburg and Red Grooms combined performance art with sculpture in enormous installations that celebrated Manhattan's buildings and crowds. The assemblage work of Jasper Johns and Robert Rauschenberg asserted that anything could become art: American flags to city dirt. The most eager celebrity of all, Andy Warhol, declared his New York studio a "factory," let workers produce many of his silkscreen prints, and ran an ad offering to sign anything for money. Once inaccessible, art became identifiable, reproducible, and, most of all, purchasable.

Left: Masterpiece by Roy Lichtenstein, 1962. Private collection, New York, © Estate of Roy Lichtenstein. Above: Savarin Can by Jasper Johns, 1960. Philadelphia Museum of Art/VAGA, NY. Opposite

above: Autumn Rhythm (Number 30) by Jackson Pollock, 1950. Metropolitan Museum of Art. Opposite below: Yellow Band by Mark Rothko, 1956. Sheldon Memorial Art Gallery, University of Nebraska, Lincoln

Untitled. Photograph by Cindy Sherman, 1979. Sherman's photographs play with identity and masquerade. *Courtesy the artist and Metro Pictures. Below: #264 (View A) by Jessica Stockholder, 1996. Stockholder's site-specific installations are both formally elegant and exuberantly improvisational. Collection Art Institute of Chicago. Photo Cathy Carver, courtesy Jay Gorney Modern Art, New York*

Persistent Visions

New York's art scene has never ceased to thrive and change, with artists cutting a path through Greenwich Village, Soho, Chelsea, and the outer boroughs. There, and along the swanky 57th Street and Madison Avenue corridors, one can sample far-ranging visual delights. Canon-setting collections appear at the city's museums, steps away from cutting-edge experiments in storefront galleries and working studios. The line between these blurs at MoMA (a mid-century showcase), the Guggenheims, and the Whitney Museum of American Art. Artists also find audiences through institutions like the Dia Center for the Arts, which pioneered the move to Chelsea in 1987.

Louise Bourgeois fused personal imagery with New York's "uneasy spaces" and "lairs" in six decades of sculptural exploration. The site-specific installation art of Dan Flavin, Jessica Stockholder, and Robert Gober combines architecture and performance art, asking viewers to consider the relationship between artist and curator, viewer and participant. Other visions celebrate the individual: Cindy Sherman acts as model and artist in her stylized photographs. From paint and stone to pixels and video loops, New York remains a place where an individual vision can move multitudes—if displayed in the right gallery at the right moment.

Above: Self-Portrait by Chuck Close, 1997. Close is primarily a portraitist, known for his billboard-sized black-and-white paintings and more recently for colored canvases using a pointillist accumulation of shapes and symbols to assemble a face. *Museum of Modern Art, New York. Left: Bus Riders* by George Segal, 1962. Segal has made his evocative plaster sculptures, usually in everyday settings, for 40 years. *Hirshhorn Museum and Sculpture Garden, Washington, D.C.*

Victoria Regia (First Night Bloom) and Victoria Regia (Second Night Bloom) by Keith Edmier, 1998. *Friedrich Petzel Gallery, New York. Below: Plundering and Alone* by Mary Esch, 1997. *Bronwyn Keenan Gallery, New York*

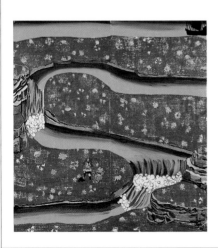

New York artists continue to explore the interplay between individual and environment as they turn to new media, including the video art of Matthew McCaslin, Keith Edmier's giant space-age flora, and the digital art assembled for the Museum of Modern Art's Website. But movements are hard to come by among new New York artists. While some turn to new technologies, others embrace canvas once again: some painting small, intimate canvases, others creating room-sized narratives in paint, photographs, and eclectic materials. Some installations celebrate spaces with their own histories, such as the one-time Queens schoolhouse P.S. 1, now an important showcase for new art, or Times Square, where Jenny Holzer's slogans vie with ads, pleading "Protect me from what I want." The new freedom extends beyond galleries to New York's countryside, in the landscapes of Vernon Dawson and the playful sculpture of Tom Otterness. ◉

Above: Cows, Rockets, Cars by Matthew McCaslin, 1997. Part of a show called "The Great American Landscape," this piece contains TV sets with video images, a clock, and a wagon. *Sandra Gering Gallery and Baumgartner Galleries, Inc. Left: Love Boat* by Polly Apfelbaum, 1998. This artist's recent works are made with scraps of velvet and other fabric scattered on a floor. *D'Amelio Terras Gallery, New York*

You Are Here

The New York Panorama at the Queens Museum of Art in Flushing Meadows is a minutely detailed scale model of the five boroughs, deviating from reality less than 1 percent. Originally conceived by Parks Commissioner Robert Moses to aid city planning, the model has been updated continuously; Staten Island was transformed from grassy suburb to urban hub, and planes now take off from a tiny LaGuardia Airport.

Above the Underground

Early New York City subway stations displayed the work of renowned architects, artists, and ceramicists, making subway travel fashionable as well as fast. Much of the original tilework remains, getting a boost from 1990s renovations. A current program, Arts for Transit, has installed a wide range of contemporary artists' work in the stations and around their street-level entrances. Among the latter is Alison Saar's *Hear the Lone Whistle Moan,* at the 125th Street Station.

An Egg for an Empire

Empire State Plaza, 98.5 acres in Albany, features one of the nation's largest collections of art in a public site. Former governor Nelson A. Rockefeller authorized the purchase, between 1966 and 1973, of 92 paintings, sculptures, and tapestries from artists working in the state. The works are sited on an enormous marble platform supporting 11 buildings, including the Empire Center at the Egg, an ovoid forum for the performing arts.

House of Glass

The Corning Museum of Glass is one of the world's great glass collections, displaying more than 27,000 individual objects and spanning 35 centuries. It is a spectular tribute to the art that made this company town famous. Visitors to the museum can tour the Steuben factory and—if their timing is right—marvel at glass-blowing demonstrations.

Lake George's "Leaping Lizard"

This gleaming 1930s speedboat, the *El Lagarto,* is among many objects that resonate with the lore of the Adirondacks to be found at the Adirondack Museum in Blue Mountain Lake. The museum also features a small but superb collection of paintings on Adirondack subjects, a luxurious private railroad car from the days of the "great camps," and other displays that bring the region and its history to life.

"The Two-Wheeled Velocipede"

A bicycle craze swept America in the 1890s, changing fashions, promoting exercise, and contributing to the growth of advertising. The social effects of the bicycle share a seat with the genuine article, displayed in many forms at the Burgwardt Bicycle Museum in Orchard Park. Visitors can mount an early high-wheel model or ponder experiments in aerodynamics, pneumatics, even aquatics.

Great People

A selective listing of native New Yorkers, focusing on the arts.

Edward Hopper (1882–1967), realist painter of city loneliness and beauty, born in Nyack

Woody Allen (b. 1935), filmmaker, comedian, New York City's most visible neurotic

Joan Baez (b. 1941), folksinger and activist

James Baldwin (1924–1987), author of *Go Tell It on the Mountain* and other classics

Lucille Ball (1911–1989), red-headed fireball of TV fame

L. Frank Baum (1856–1919), creator of *The Wizard of Oz*, born in Chittenango

Humphrey Bogart (1899–1957), actor, born in New York City

Matthew Brady (1823–1896), America's pioneer photographer

George Burns (1896–1996), half of celebrated comedy team with Gracie Allen

Maria Callas (1923–1977), diva

Cab Calloway (b. 1907), big-band leader and singer, born in Rochester

Aaron Copland (1900–1990), composer who brought American rhythms to classical music

Jasper Cropsey (1823–1900), one of the few native-born artists of the Hudson River School

E. L. Doctorow (b. 1931), novelist whose plots often center on New York history

George Gershwin (1898–1937), composer of rhythmic genius

Oscar Hammerstein II (1895–1960), lyricist of many Broadway hits

Washington Irving (1783–1859), creator of Rip Van Winkle and other upstate legends

Henry James (1843–1916), novelist whose stories revisit the New York of his childhood

William Kennedy (b. 1928), author of *Ironweed* and other novels set in his native Albany

Herman Melville (1819–1891), author of *Moby Dick*

Arthur Miller (b. 1915), playwright; best known for *Death of a Salesman*

Barnett Newman (1905–1970), leading Abstract Expressionist

Eugene O'Neill (1888–1953), Nobel-winning playwright

Margaret Sanger (1883–1966), family-planning pioneer, born in Corning

Jerry Seinfeld (b. 1955), comedian of New York singles' angst

Louis Comfort Tiffany (1848–1933), stained glass artist, pioneer of Art Nouveau

Edith Wharton (1862–1937), chronicler of "Old New York"

Walt Whitman (1819–1892), America's all-embracing poet, born on Long Island

...and Great Places

Some interesting derivations of New York place names.

Adirondack The Algonquian dubbed their Iroquois enemies "tree-eaters" (rat-iron-tacks).

Bogota One of several names suggesting tropical dreams, along with Bombay and Mexico, all in the frozen North Country.

Bronx For Jonas Bronck, a Dane. The inspiration for an Ogden Nash couplet: "The Bronx?/No, thonx."

Brooklyn For the Dutch city Breukelen, as Harlem commemorates the Dutch Haerlem.

Catskill Mountains Originally Kaaterskill, from the Dutch "kill" (creek) and the woodland's great wildcats.

Cattaraugus A town, creek, and county, meaning "stinking shore" (Iroquois).

Kayaderosseras Iroquois, meaning "lake country."

Lawyersville A good destination (in Schoharie County) for crooks who find no luck in **Protection** (Erie County).

Mad Nan's Neck First English name for today's Great Neck, Long Island. "Neck" is from the Native American "naiack"(point or corner), which also yields Nyack.

Manhattan Probably from the Algonquian *manna-hatta,* for either "hilly island" or "place of general intoxication."

Oneida "People of the sacred stone," one of five original Iroquois nations. All are preserved in New York county names.

Oneonta "Stony place" (Iroquois). Related to Ossining: "stone upon stone," and its infamous prison, Sing-Sing.

Paumanack Algonquian name for Long Island, meaning "land of tribute"; Walt Whitman wanted to see it reinstated.

Pompey One of many classical names assigned in 1789 to the Military Tract reserved for veterans of the Revolution. Others include Athens, Babylon, Carthage, Cicero, Egypt, and Troy.

Purgatory Swamp "Easy to git in, hard to git out," as the locals say.

Spuyten Duyvil A creek that runs between Manhattan and The Bronx, into the Hudson. The name comes from a Dutch story in which the hero swims a channel "to spite the devil."

Ticonderoga "Place of sounding waters," a poetic way of saying "noisy."

Wappinger "East lands," a tribe living to the east of the Mohawk, the easternmost tribe of Iroquois.

Kinderhook Hudson Valley village ("children's corner," from the Dutch). Birthplace of President Martin Van Buren, whose campaign slogan proclaiming him "Old Kinderhook" became the word heard round the world: O.K.

NEW YORK BY THE SEASONS
A Perennial Calendar of Events and Festivals

Here is a selective listing of events that take place each year in the months noted; we suggest calling ahead to local chambers of commerce for dates and details.

January

Apalachin
Winter Carnival

Wappingers Falls
Nature at Stony Kill Farm
Weekend programs include
Exploring on Snowshoes,
Winter Botany, Owl Search.

February

Apalachin
Winter Birding Weekend

Halsey Valley
Ice-Cutting Festival
Celebrates traditional art of ice-
cutting and storage.

March

Marathon, Cortland County
Central New York Maple Festival
Celebration of tree-tapping;
crafts show, syrups and candies,
tours of the Maple Museum.

Tioga County
Daffodil Festival
Flower and crafts show benefits
American Cancer Society.

April

Franklinville
Western New York Maple Festival
Arts, crafts, antiques, edibles.

Nyack
Springfest
Features a juried crafts show.

Saratoga Springs
*Northeastern Wood Workers
Association Show*

May

Brooklyn
Blessing of the Fishing Fleet
For a bountiful spring harvest.

Huntington
*Walt Whitman Birthday
Celebration*
At the poet's birthplace.

Kingston
Shad Festival
Shad-roe dinners complete a
day of exhibits and boat-rides.

North Creek
Hudson River Whitewater Derby
Kayak and canoe races; for over
40 years.

Rochester
Lilac Festival
Arts, music, and a parade welcome blossoms on 1,200 lilac
bushes of 500 varieties.

Seneca Lake
National Lake Trout Derby
Prizes up to $25,000.

June

Auburn
Dairy and Old Ways Day
Churning, ice-cream making,
and log cutting.

Niagara Falls
Project Vow Renewal
Renew your wedding vows in
the world's largest ceremony.

Rochester
Maplewood Rose Festival
Celebration of the state flower,
featuring 5,000 rose varieties.

Saratoga
Newport Jazz Festival
At the outdoor Saratoga
Performing Arts Center.

Sterling
Renaissance Festival
Runs for 7 weekends; employs
600 actors.

July

Albany and Grafton
Empire State Games
Features canoeing, kayaking,
and other summer sports.

Ancramdale
Winterhawk Bluegrass Festival

Clayton
Decoy and Wildlife Art Show
Exhibits, demonstrations.

Cooperstown
Glimmerglass Opera Festival

Morristown
Quilting by the Lake
Workshops and a show on the shores of Black Lake.

Rochester
Annual Corn Hill Arts Festival
Gathers 500 artists in a 19th-century neighborhood.

Syracuse
New York State Blues Festival

Thousand Islands
Fourth of July
Fireworks over Boldt Castle.

Watkins Glen
Finger Lakes Wine Festival
Thirty wineries offer tastings, seminars, music, and arts.

August

Bolton Landing
Barbershop Quartet Festival
Showcases more than 100 quartets from around the world.

Boonville
NYS Woodsmen's Field Day
For more than 50 years; a celebration of forestry.

Gerry
Gerry Rodeo
Longest-running rodeo east of the Mississippi.

Oyster Bay
Long Island Summer Jazz Festival

Southhampton
Shinnecock Pow Wow
Traditional ceremonial.

Syracuse
The Great New York State Fair
Queen of the state's many agricultural celebrations.

Watkins Glen
The Bud in the Glen
NASCAR and CSAA auto races at world-famous racetrack.

September

Blue Mountain Lake
Rustic Furniture Fair
More than 40 furniture makers show one-of-a-kind designs.

Palmyra
Canaltown Days
Arts and crafts, antiques, parades.

October

Hudson
Arts Walk
Columbia County artists open their galleries to the public.

Hyde Park
Artists in the Garden
Art show in the Vanderbilt Mansion's Italian garden.

Ithaca
Book Sale
Third-largest book sale in U.S.

Lewis County
Fall Foliage Drive-It-Yourself Tour

Oyster Bay
Oyster Festival

Rhinebeck
Sheep and Wool Festival
Showcases ewes, llamas, alpacas, and sheepdogs, plus fleece sale.

Craft Fair
Premier location for high-end crafts; also in June.

Wolcott
Wolcott Apple Harvest
Farmers market, pie contest, chariot races, music.

November

Newtonville
Hudson—Mohawk Weaver's Guild Exhibit
Show and sale; demonstrations.

Various locations
Hudson Valley Storytelling Festival
Weekend of celebrating and teaching the art of storytelling; in Dutchess County.

Holiday crafts fairs begin throughout the state

December

Dutchess County
Roosevelt House Tours
Tour FDR's former home (Springwood), the birthplace of Eleanor Roosevelt (Val-Kill), and their joint estate (Hyde Park), decorated for the season.

Onondaga
Lights on the Lake Festival
Two-mile, drive-through holiday lights show.

Tarrytown
Candlelight Tours
Tours of historic Hudson Valley mansions include Lyndhurst, Philipsburg Manor, Van Cortland Manor, and Sunnyside.

WHERE TO GO
Museums, Attractions, Gardens, and Other Arts Resources

Call for seasons and hours when open.

Museums

ALBRIGHT-KNOX ART GALLERY
1285 Elmwood Ave., Buffalo, 716-882-8700
First U.S. museum to purchase works by Matisse and Picasso remains a center for contemporary art.

AMERICAN CRAFT MUSEUM
40 W. 53d St., Manhattan, 212-956-6047
Spectacular contemporary works in glass, weaving, and ceramics. Also offers quilting masterworks and classes for fans of American crafts.

AMERICAN MUSEUM OF NATURAL HISTORY
Central Park West at 79th St., Manhattan, 212-769-5100
Houses the Hayden Planetarium (reopens after renovations in 2000), countless minerals, gems, fossils, and dinosaur bones. A favorite with kids of all ages.

ASIA SOCIETY GALLERY
725 Park Ave. at 70th St., Manhattan, 212-517-NEWS
The Rockefeller collection of Asian art.

BROOKLYN MUSEUM OF ART
200 Eastern Parkway, Brooklyn, 718-638-5000
Among the world's finest collections of classical and ancient art in a landmark Beaux-Arts building.

CHILDREN'S MUSEUM OF MANHATTAN
212-W. 83rd St., Manhattan, 212-721-1234
Four floors of noisy, messy, artful fun, with a Dr. Seuss exhibit on the ground floor.

THE CLOISTERS
Fort Tryon Park, Manhattan
The medieval collections of the Metropolitan Museum, hand-picked by John D. Rockefeller, reside at this astonishing castle overlooking the Hudson.

COOPER-HEWITT, NATIONAL DESIGN MUSEUM
2 E. 91st St., Manhattan, 212-860-6898
The one-time Andrew Carnegie residence now devotes three floors to the design collections of the Smithsonian Institution, from commercial to high art.

CORNING MUSEUM OF GLASS
One Museum Way, Corning
One of the world's great glass collections; more than 27,000 individual objects spanning 35 centuries.

THE DIA CENTER FOR THE ARTS
548 and 545 W. 22nd Sts., Manhattan, 212-989-5912
One of the first nonprofit alternative spaces for new art; remains a center for the conceptual set.

EL MUSEO DEL BARRIO
1230 Fifth Ave. at 104th St., Manhattan, 212-831-7272
This "neighborhood museum" celebrates the richness of Latin arts in the Americas.

ELLIS ISLAND MUSEUM OF IMMIGRATION
Ellis Island, 212-363-7620
Reopened after sweeping renovation, it offers interactive exhibits and eloquent photographs of the peopling of America.

FARMER'S MUSEUM
Lake Road, Rt. 80, Cooperstown
One of the country's first outdoor museums recreates an agricultural main street.

FASHION INSTITUTE OF TECHNOLOGY
Seventh Ave. (26th and 28th Sts.), Manhattan, 212-760-7760
An elite school for aspiring designers in the heart of the garment district; presents occasional exhibits.

THE FRICK COLLECTION
1 East 70th St., Manhattan, 212-288-0700
Fifth Avenue mansion decorated in wall-to-wall Old
Masters and Renaissance bronze treasures.

SOLOMON R. GUGGENHEIM MUSEUM
1071 Fifth Ave. at 82nd St., Manhattan, 212-423-3500

GUGGENHEIM MUSEUM SOHO
575 Broadway at Prince St., Manhattan, 212-423-3500
The uptown museum is best known for Frank Lloyd
Wright's spiraling design and its definitive Kandinsky
collection, while the newer downtown Guggenheim
highlights video and multimedia exhibitions.

JEWISH MUSEUM
1109 Fifth Ave. at 92nd St., Manhattan, 212-423-3200
Provocative displays range from the Holocaust to
Jewish humor on American TV.

METROPOLITAN MUSEUM OF ART
1000 Fifth Ave. at 82nd St., Manhattan, 212-535-7710
The grande dame of New York's museums, with
strong collections of European , American, and
ancient art; also houses the Costume Institute.

MUSEUM OF MODERN ART (MOMA)
11 W. 53d St., Manhattan, 212-708-9480
World's most comprehensive survey of 20th-century
art in all media; its sculpture garden is a refuge.

MUSEUM OF THE CITY OF NEW YORK
1220 Fifth Ave., Manhattan 212-534-1672
Only museum devoted to the history of New York City.

NATIONAL MUSEUM OF THE AMERICAN INDIAN
*U.S. Customs House, One Bowling Green, Manhattan
212-668-6624*
Assembles artifacts from Algonquian and Iroquois
tribes, as well as multimedia exhibits.

STORM KING ART CENTER
Old Pleasant Hill Road, Mountainville, 914-534-3115
The Hudson River and mountains frame this gallery-
on-a-hillside, a sculpture park that exhibits works by
the great names in postwar sculpture.

P.S. 1 CONTEMPORARY ART CENTER
22-25 Jackson Ave., Long Island City, 718-784-2084
A one-time schoolhouse transformed to a sunny,
high-ceilinged showcase for new art.

WHITNEY MUSEUM OF AMERICAN ART
945 Madison Ave. at 75th St., 212-570-3600
Permanent and rotating exhibits of American art in
an award-winning Marcel Breuer building. New
directions are showcased in the often controversial
Whitney Biennial.

Attractions

THE APOLLO
253 West 125th St., Manhattan, 212-749-5838
The beginning of the road for many African-
American superstars and a destination for jazz and
blues lovers worldwide.

NATIONAL BASEBALL HALL OF FAME AND MUSEUM
25 Main St., Cooperstown, 607-547-7200
Honors the careers of baseball's greats and recaps the
raucous history of America's pastime.

BRONX ZOO AND NATURE PRESERVE
*Fordham Rd. and Bronx River Parkway, Bronx,
718-367-1010*
Snow leopards, rare Père David deer, baboons, and
elephants roam in compassionate and grassy sur-
roundings.

CHAUTAUQUA INSTITUTION, CHAUTAUQUA
America's original self-improvement community
offers summer program of seminars and symphonies.

LAKE PLACID OLYMPIC MUSEUM
Lake Placid

The Olympic Museum contains memorabilia and exhibits from the 1932 and 1980 Winter Games.

NATIONAL SOARING MUSEUM
Harris Hill Road, Elmira, 607-734-3128.

At the the Finger Lakes' hang-gliding nexus, this museum celebrates the history of motorless flight.

SARATOGA RACE COURSE
Union Ave., Saratoga Springs, 518-584-6200

Bring your best hat to the nation's oldest thoroughbred track; or dress down for an outdoor jazz or ballet concert at the Saratoga Performing Arts Center.

Homes and Gardens

HYDE PARK, SPRINGWOOD, VAL-KILL
Dutchess County, 800-FDR-VISIT

FDR grew up at Springwood, a Georgian mansion high above the Hudson, and lived with his family at Hyde Park. Eleanor moved to Val-Kill after his death.

OLANA
Hudson

Overlooking the Hudson and flanked by gardens and a lake, painter Frederic Church's Persian-style castle houses works by Church and Thomas Cole.

ROSE HILL MANSION
Rt. 96A, Geneva, 315-789-3848

Greek Revival mansion contains an impressive collection of Empire-stye furniture.

SAGAMORE HILL
20 Sagamore Rd., Oyster Bay, 516-922-4447

Teddy Roosevelt summered here; the National Park Service has since taken over management.

SONNENBERG MANSION AND GARDEN ESTATE
151 Charlotte St., Canandaigua

The Smithsonian calls this former home of banker Frederick Ferris Thompson, "one of the most magnificent late-Victorian gardens ever created in America."

SUNNYSIDE
Tarrytown, 914-631-8200

Washington Irving's whimsical farmhouse estate contains some of the writer's own furniture.

WAVE HILL
Riverdale, 718-549-3200

Residents of this striking Greek Revival mansion overlooking the Hudson have included Mark Twain, Theodore Roosevelt, and Arturo Toscanini.

WHITMAN BIRTHPLACE
246 Old Walt Whitman Rd., Huntington Station, 516-427-5240

Walt Whitman's birthplace retains the hand-hewn feel of another age.

Other Resources

NEW YORK PUBLIC LIBRARY
Fifth Ave. at 42nd St., Manhattan 212-869-8069

One of the world's great research libraries, with assorted treasures on public view.

NEW YORK STATE MUSEUM
Madison Ave., Albany, 518-474-8577.

The oldest and largest state museum in the country captures the Empire State's diversity.

SCHOMBURG CENTER FOR RESEARCH IN BLACK CULTURE
515 Malcolm X Blvd. at 135th St., Manhattan, 212-491-2200.

The foremost collection of books, manuscripts, recordings, videos, and prints of the African diaspora.

CREDITS

The authors have made every effort to reach copyright holders of text and owners of illustrations, and wish to thank those individuals and institutions that permitted the reprinting of text or the reproduction of works in their collections. Those credits not listed in the captions are provided below. References are to page numbers; the designations *a*, *b*, and *c* indicate position of illustrations on pages.

Text

Aperture Foundation: Copyright © Alfred Stieglitz, "One Day During the Winter Season," *Masters of Photography No. 6*. Aperture: New York, NY 1989.

Elizabeth Barnett: "Recuerdo" by Edna St. Vincent Millay. From *Collected Poems*, HarperCollins. Copyright © 1922, 1950 by Edna St. Vincent Millay.

George Braziller, Inc.: *The Streamlined Decade* by Donald Bush. Copyright © 1975 by Donald Bush.

Facts on File, Inc.: From *Ellis Island Interviews* by Peter Coan. Copyright © 1997 by Peter Coan. Reprinted by permission of Facts On File, Inc.

Harcourt & Brace: *It Happened in Brooklyn* by Myrna Frommer. Copyright © 1993 by Harvey Frommer and Myrna Katz Frommer. Reprinted by permission of the publisher.

HarperCollins Publishers, Inc.: *The Autobiography of Eleanor Roosevelt*. Copyright © 1937, 1949, 1958, 1960, 1961 by Anna Eleanor Roosevelt, © 1958 by Curtis Publishing Co. Reprinted by permission of the publisher.

International Creative Management: *Here Is New York* by E. B. White. Copyright © 1949 by E. B. White.

New Directions Publishing Corp.: From *The Crack–up* by F. Scott Fitzgerald. Copyright © 1945 by J. Laughlin Publishers. Reprinted by permission of New Directions.

Random House, Inc.: *Act One: An Autobiography* by Moss Hart. Copyright © 1959 by Kathryn Carlisle Hart and Joseph M. Hyman, trustees. By permission of the publisher.

Simon & Schuster: From *The Age of Innocence* by Edith Wharton. Copyright © 1920 by D. Appleton and Company, renewed 1948 by William R. Tyler. Excerpted by permission of Scribner, a division of Simon & Schuster, from *The Great Gatsby* (authorized text) by F. Scott Fitzgerald. Copyright © 1925 Charles Scribner's Sons. Copyright

renewed 1953 by Frances Scott Fitzgerald Lanahan. Copyright © 1991, 1992 by Eleanor Lanahan, Matthew J. Bruccoli and Samuel J. Lanahan as Trustees u/a dated 7/3/75, created by Frances Scott Fitzgerald Smith.

White Pine Press: "I am turtle, and my tribes remain forever" by Peter Blue Cloud from *A Clan of Many Nations: Selected Poems, 1969-1992*. Copyright © 1993. Reprinted with the permission of White Pine Press, Fredonia, NY.

W. W. Norton & Co., Inc.: *The Poems of Hart Crane* by Hart Crane. Copyright © 1986 by Liveright Publishing Corp. Reprinted by permission of W. W. Norton & Co., Inc. Ogden Nash poem from *The New Yorker*, May 3, 1930. Reprinted by permission of Curtis Brown, Ltd.

Illustrations

ADIRONDACK MUSEUM: **27b** *Schroon Lake*. Oil on canvas. 32½ x 31"; **69b**; AMERICA HURRAH ARCHIVE: **1**; **42b**; **53** *The Oliver M. Pettit*. Oil on canvas. 22 x 48"; **68b**; AMERICAN INDIAN CONTEMPORARY ARTS: **56b** *My Dog Spot*. Oil on plastic; ARCHIVE OF AMERICAN GARDENS, SMITHSONIAN INSTITUTION: **11**, **72b**; ART INSTITUTE OF CHICAGO: **70a** *Terrace Bridge*. Watercolor. 15¼ x 22¼"; **98b** Installation. Acrylic paint, oil paint on glass, wooden shingles, wire mesh, green wire, silicon caulking, acrylic yarn, scarf, thread, and hardware. Photo courtesy Jay Gorney Modern Art; BERRY-HILL GALLERIES: **29** *A Sketch of Montauk Light*. Oil on canvas. 8¼ x 18⅜"; BROOKLYN MUSEUM OF ART: **5** *Bathing at Bellport, Long Island*. Oil on canvas. 26 x 32"; COOPER-HEWITT, NATIONAL DESIGN MUSEUM, SMITHSONIAN INSTITUTION: **73** *Olana from the Southwest*. Oil on thin board. 12³⁄₁₆ x 9½". Gift of Louis P. Church, 1917-4-666; CORCORAN GALLERY OF ART: **21** *Niagara*. Oil on canvas. 27¾ x 36½". Museum purchase, gallery fund; **23** *Hudson River Logging*. Watercolor. 14 x 20⅝". Museum purchase; D'AMELIO TERRAS GALLERY: **101b** *Love Boat*. Velvet and dye installation; FISK UNIVERSITY ART GALLERIES: **49** *Radiator Building*. Oil on canvas. 48 x 30"; SANDRA GERING GALLERY AND BAUMGARTNER GALLERIES, INC.: **101a** *Cows, Rockets, Cars*. Mixed media; ESTATE OF KEITH HARING: **55a** *Untitled*. Subway drawing, Chalk on paper, fiberglass frame. 87¼ x 45¼"; HIRSHORN MUSEUM AND SCULPTURE GARDEN, SMITHSONIAN INSTITUTION: **99b** *Bus Riders*. Plaster, cotton gauze, steel, wood, and vinyl. 70 x 42½ x 90¾"; BRONWYN KEENAN GALLERY: **100b** *Plundering and Alone*.

Acrylic on paper. 62 x 59"; LIBRARY OF CONGRESS: **10, 19b** Woodstock; **32** *Arrival of the Half-Moon.* 40 x 30"; **60; 89a;** ESTATE OF ROY LICHTENSTEIN: **97a** *Masterpiece.* Oil on canvas. 54 x 54"; MAIER MUSEUM OF ART: **43** *Men of the Docks.* Oil on canvas. 45 x 63½"; MARLBOROUGH GALLERY: **2** *Looking Along Broadway.* Mixed media. 71 x 63¾ x 28¾"; THE METROPOLITAN MUSEUM OF ART: **71a** Gift of Louis Comfort Tiffany Foundation, 1951. (51.121.17). Photograph © 1991 The Metropolitan Museum of Art; **96a** *Autumn Rhythm.* Oil on canvas. 8'9 x 17'3". George A. Hearn Fund, 1957 (57.92). Photograph © 1998 The Metropolitan Museum of Art; MUSEUM OF AMERICAN FOLK ART, NY: **51a** *Whosoever Reports a Thing.* Acrylic on canvas. 24 x 30". Gift of a friend of the museum; MUSEUM OF MODERN ART, NY: **93** *Flatiron Building.* Gravure on vellum. 12⅞ x 6⅝"; **94b** *Broadway Boogie Woogie.* Oil on canvas. 50 x 50"; MUSEUM OF THE CITY OF NEW YORK: **16a** *Unveiling the Statue of Liberty.* Oil on canvas. 39½ x 49½". J. Clarence Davies Collection; **35a** *Alexander Hamilton.* Oil on canvas. 17¾ x 13¾"; **35b** Evacuation Day stoneware. Gift of Mr. Charles A. Dana, Jr.; **36** Deck figure. Carved wood. 78 x 24". Gift of Augustus Van Horne Ellis; **36-37** *Erie Canal Celebration.* Oil on canvas. 45 x 24". Anonymous gift; **38** *Bay and Harbor of New York.* Oil on canvas. 8'2 x 16'6". Gift of Mrs. Robert M. Littlejohn; **41b** *The Ice Cart.* Watercolor. 10¼ x 14"; **50a** *Trinity Church.* Lithograph. 22 x 15⅛". J. Clarence Davies Collection; **52a** *De Witt Clinton.* Oil on canvas. 48 x 36". Gift of Mrs. Leonard W. Bonney; **55b** *Seventh Avenue Subway.* Oil on panel. 36 x 22". Gift of James W. Kerr; **56a** *Rail Road Bridge.* Oil on canvas. 15⅞ x 11⅞". The Harry T. Peters Collection; **59a; 61b; 62** *Union Square.* Oil on canvas. 48 x 37". Gift of Peter Hopkins; **71b** Bedroom. Gift of John D. Rockefeller, Jr.; **74a** *Steeplechase Park.* Oil on canvas. 51 x 80". Gift of Mrs. George C. Tilyou; **82a** *Chinese Theater.* Oil on canvas. 18 x 26". The Robert R. Preato Collection; **88a** *George Gershwin.* Oil on canvas. 45 x 55". Gift of Max D. Levy; NATIONAL GALLERY OF ART: **24** *The Hudson Valley, Sunset.* Oil on canvas. 22 x 30"; **27a** *Autumn—On the Hudson River.* Oil on canvas. 60" x 9'. Gift of the Avalon Foundation, © 1998 Board of Trustees; NATIONAL GEOGRAPHIC IMAGE COLLECTION: **12a** Flag. Marilyn Dye Smith; **12b** Bluebird and rose. Robert E. Hynes, **17a, 34** *General Burgoyne.* Oil on canvas. 12 x 18'; NATIONAL MUSEUM OF AMERICAN ART/ART RESOURCE: **25** *Storm King.* Oil on canvas. 32 x 60". Gift of John Gellatly; **58** *Skating in Central Park.* Oil on canvas. 33⅞ x 48½"; **91a** *Les Fétiches.* Oil on canvas. 25½ x 21¼"; **94a** *Artists on WPA.* Oil on canvas. 36⅛ x 42⅛"; **95** *Third Avenue.* Oil on canvas 36 x 30⅛"; NATIONAL PORTRAIT GALLERY/ART RESOURCE: **64a** *Elizabeth Cady Stanton.* Oil on canvas. 39¾ x 32½"; **70b** *Edith Wharton.* Oil on canvas. 28½ x 21½"; **78b** *Edna St. Vincent Millay.* Oil on canvas. 30 x 25"; **80b** *Walt Whitman.* Platinum print. 4¾ x 3⅞"; **104;** THE NEW-YORK HISTORICAL SOCIETY: **33a** *Peter Stuyvesant.* Oil on wood panel. 22½ x 17½"; **40a** *Tontine Coffee House.* Oil on canvas. 42¼ x 64¼"; **52b** *Erie Canal.* Watercolor on paper. 9½ x 13½"; **63a;** NEW YORK STATE HISTORICAL ASSOCIATION, COOPERSTOWN: **30b; 33b** *Van Bergen Overmantel.* Oil on wood. 15¼ x 74¾". **42a** *Cider Making.* Oil on canvas. 17⅛ x 27½"; ONONDAGA HISTORICAL ASSOCIATION: **54a** *Clinton Square, 1871.* Oil on canvas. 40⅛ x 56⅜"; PERFORMING ARTS RESEARCH CENTER, NY PUBLIC LIBRARY: **82b;** FRIEDRICH PETZAL GALLERY: **100a** *Victoria Regia.* Both 9'4 x 10'8 x 11'1"; PHILADELPHIA MUSEUM OF ART/VAGA, NY: **97a** *Savarin Can.* Bronze. Lent by the artist; JIM PRIGOFF: **65b;** NORMAN ROCKWELL FAMILY TRUST/DRAPER VISUAL ARTS: **79b** *Ichabod Crane.* Oil on canvas. 38 x 24"; SCHOMBURG CENTER FOR RESEARCH IN BLACK CULTURE, NY PUBLIC LIBRARY: **90a** *Jenkin's Band.* Oil on canvas. 30 x 30". SHELDON MEMORIAL ART GALLERY: **92** *Room in New York.* Oil on canvas. 29 x 36". F. M. Hall Collection; **96b** *Yellow Band.* Oil on canvas. 7'2 x 6'8". Thomas C. Woods Memorial; SMITHSONIAN INSTITUTION: **11c; 47b;** STORM KING ART CENTER, MOUNTAINVILLE, NY: **59b** *Voltron XX.* Steel. 62¼ x 37½ x 26½". Gift of the Ralph E. Ogden Foundation, Inc.; VAGA, INC.: **9** *Roosevelt Mural.* Tempera on board. 20 x 29". © Estate of Ben Shahn; WHITNEY MUSEUM OF AMERICAN ART: **57** *The Brooklyn Bridge.* Oil on canvas. 70 x 42". Museum purchase; PACE WILDENSTEIN GALLERY: **99a** *Self Portrait.* Oil on canvas. 8'6" x 7'.

Acknowledgments

Walking Stick Press wishes to thank our project staff: Miriam Lewis, Kina Sullivan, Thérèse Martin, Laurie Donaldson, Lani Gallegos, Nancy Barnes, Mark Woodworth, and Adam Ling. For other assistance with *New York,* we are especially grateful to: Laurel Anderson, Lindsay Kefauver, Dave Stevenson, Natalie Goldstein, the staff of the Museum of the City of New York, Claudia Goldstein at Art Resource, Lisa Vasquez at Corbis/ Bettmann, Joel Kopp of America Hurrah, John Kuss at the New-York Historical Society, the Adirondack Museum, the New York State Historical Association, and New York Times Pictures.